Pillow
TALK

Other Books by Karen Linamen

The Parent Warrior: Doing Spiritual Battle for Your Children

Working Women, Workable Lives, with Linda Holland

Deadly Secrets, with Keith Wall

The Intimate Marriage from A to Z

Karen Scalf Linamen

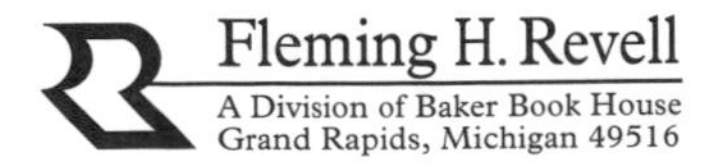

Published by Fleming H. Revell
a division of Baker Book House Company
P.O. Box 6287, Grand Rapids, MI 49516-6287

Printed in the United States of America

Library of Congress Cataloging-in-Publication Data

Linamen, Karen Scalf, 1960–
Pillow talk : the intimate marriage from A to Z / Karen Scalf Linamen
p. cm.
ISBN 0-8007-1730-9 (cloth)
1. Sex instruction for women. 2. Sex in marriage. 3. Sex—Religious aspects—Christianity. 4. Women—Sexual behavior. 5. Christian women—Conduct of life. 6. Communication in marriage. I. Title.
HQ46.L56 1996
613.9.'6'082—dc20 96-20791

Contents

Dedication

I think it might be some sort of unwritten publishing faux pas when your dedication page rivals your first chapter in length, but bear with me.

As I was busy writing this book for women everywhere, I knew that I wanted to dedicate it to a small group of special women—women in my family—who have enriched my life in an immeasurable fashion. Somewhere I once heard the phrase "many strong and beautiful women," and it made me think immediately of the grandmothers, aunts, sisters, cousins, and incredible mother with whom I have been blessed. Funny, wise, and godly women all, this book is dedicated to . . .

Minnie Scalf and Rose Shakarian who—as grandmothers and as godly women—have always been bright lights and shining stars in my life. "Mamaw" and "Momie," you are precious to me and I love you both.

My sister Renee Berge, whose seafood fettucini is to die for. I also admire her mettle; as a military wife and mother of two preschoolers, Renee rises to the challenges around her with tenacity and style.

Aunt Jeanette Sharp, one of my all-time favorite people, is the owner of a quick wit and an even quicker smile. Most of all, she's someone I've always admired and loved for her transparency and golden heart.

Mother-in-law Maxine Linamen. A citizen of heaven for nearly thirteen years, she spent much of her time here on earth loving and raising two little boys, one of whom grew up to be my husband. Her generous spirit and her smile knew no strangers, and we miss her still.

Mother-in-law Jan Linamen. Twelve years ago she gave new life to Dad Linamen, and gave the rest of us someone to love and adore. I cherish her friendship and continue to be inspired by her example.

Aunt Debbie Shakarian, a strong woman of integrity, whose Christmas fudge happens to be the best this side of heaven (I don't think I'm taking theological license here: Can anyone really doubt there will be chocolate in heaven?), and Aunt Vangie Shakarian, whose welcoming smile and warm hospitality contributed to many of my best childhood memories.

Sister-in-law Debbie Linamen, who has worth and sparkle and wisdom beyond measure.

Grandma Eyla Linamen, a godly matriarch with a spicy personality, who has spent her life in loving service to her family.

My sister Michelle Scalf. Who says God can't economize? In Michelle he's given me a best friend, mentor, philosopher, sister, personal comedienne, and partner-in-mischief all rolled into one.

And to my mother, Geri Shakarian Scalf. Her insights and wisdom continue to amaze me, while her calm and gracious demeanor still manage to provide a soothing antidote to many of the stresses in my life. If I can be half the mother to my own precious daughters, they will be fortunate girls indeed.

Acknowledgments

Kudos to one terrific friend and editor Linda Holland, as well as others at Baker/Revell who worked hard to make this book a reality. Bill Petersen comes to mind, as does Sheila Ingram, Jane Schrier, and the editorial staff, as well as Twila Bennett, Lori Craker, Lisa Hovingh, and Marci DeVries. I'm also grateful to Liz Duckworth for agreeing to take on this manuscript and for the fine editing she provided. In addition, Ramona Tucker at *Today's Christian Woman* deserves applause for prompting me to consider a project along these lines to begin with.

My thanks also to Dr. Robert Holmes, who shined a bright light in a dark place and helped me recover some important things I had lost, my pen being among them.

And I certainly can't forget all the family members, close friends, and acquaintances to whom I promised anonymity in return for wonderful stories and insights about the mysteries of love and marriage. I'd list all your names here, but then you wouldn't be very anonymous, would you?

And finally, my gratitude belongs to my husband, Larry: Thank you for the pep talks and back rubs and for the way you brag about my books to total strangers, and for being the one I love and want to grow old with as we practice our ABCs all the way into our golden years.

Introduction

In the past two years, the concept for this book has worn many faces. One thing, however, has remained constant. It didn't matter whether I was kicking around the idea of an article, a monthly magazine column, or a full-fledged book—wherever I talked about an ABC approach to sex and intimacy in marriage, women around me brightened and asked where they could get in line for the first copy.

We all want better marriages, don't we? More romance, better sex, greater emotional intimacy, clearer communication. But when it comes to finding road-tested, practical ideas on how to make that happen, well . . . that's not always as easy as it sounds!

I remember when I became engaged to be married at twenty-one. My mom and I had already shared many insightful conversations about sexual and emotional intimacy in marriage. Upon my engagement she began to wrap up her advice to me, providing me with three books on marriage. As a young woman about to embark on the adventure of a lifetime, I found the books very helpful, but I also experienced no small amount of trepidation as I surveyed the hundreds of pages of small type penned by pastors, doctors, and therapists. I began to wonder: Was my sexuality really all that complicated?

Fifteen years, two mortgages, and two kids later, I understand a few things better than I did as a starry-eyed bride. I know now that sexual and emotional intimacy in marriage is, at the same time, both more and less complex than I had originally feared. Oh, there's some mystery to it, to be sure. And it doesn't happen quite as effortlessly as it does on TV, requiring instead a goodly amount of dedication and attention. But, basically, it's a lot simpler than programming the VCR or getting your kids to put the new roll of toilet paper on the spindle.

All of which, somehow, brought me to the idea of an alphabet book for women. What better way could there be to explore the simple mysteries of marriage? An ABC book, after all, speaks volumes about the simplicity of the matter, while giving ample opportunity to examine the complexities in a generous number of chapters.

And when it came time to plan the content of those chapters, I knew that my message had to be as unique as my format. As I considered what I wish I had known as a newlywed, what I've learned—and have yet to learn!—as an experienced wife and mother, and what I wanted to write about as an author, the following ideas emerged:

For starters, I knew I wanted something written woman to woman. Couple books are fine, but I pictured something created specifically with the problems, perspectives, and passions of a '90s woman in mind.

I wanted something written by an average Joan. Without belittling the contribution of pastors, counselors, and doctors, I wanted to hear some advice for married women from—what a concept!—a married woman.

I wanted something fun to read. No diagrams or technical descriptions for me! I wanted something conversational and lighthearted. I wanted humor. Anecdotes. Road-tested suggestions and insights coupled with a good belly laugh now and then.

In other words, I wanted something that would complement, rather than necessarily replace, textbooks written by pastors, therapists, and other professionals. I wanted something more philosophical than technical, more "common-sensical" than clinical, something that felt a little more like a kitchen-table chat with a good friend and a little less like my annual visit to the gynecologist.

What you are holding in your hands is the result of that wish list, and my sincerest hope is that you have as much fun reading it as I did putting it together.

Whether you are a newlywed, a young mother, a member of the forty-something crowd, or an empty nester, I'm confident that you will benefit from the stories, interviews, and ideas in the pages of this book. What kinds of ideas? How about:

- how to fantasize about your husband in a manner that is pleasing to God and constructive for your marriage
- how to have more energy for lovemaking
- how to exercise your five senses in ways that will enhance your love life
- how to learn to accept and enjoy your body despite the flaws and imperfections that plague us all
- how to protect your marriage against outside temptations and distractions
- and much, much more

Despite tough pressures that threaten your marriage daily, despite all the scary statistics about divorces and affairs and unhappy unions, despite the fact that you can't quite remember the last time you and your husband worried about what midnight noises the kids might overhear, you *can* have a more passionate marriage.

All you have to do is know your ABCs!

Ask for What You Need in the Bedroom

There are a lot of mysteries in the world.

Stonehenge. The Black Hole. Wire hangers that procreate in dark closets.

Yes, mysteries abound. And yet we women seem to feel the need to make life, well, just a little more mysterious. Especially when it comes to our husbands.

It's true. We don't want much.

We just want them to read our minds.

This is why, when they come home from work and find themselves recipients of The Silent Treatment, they ask us what is wrong and we toss them a chilling look and say, "*You* know."

This is why, when we are given a small, intimate-looking Christmas package and unwrap the tissue to discover a new remote for the garage opener, we fume at the men who were supposed to have known about the diamond tennis bracelet we've been coveting all year. My husband always asks, "But how was I supposed to know?" I consider this a ridiculous question in light of the elephantine clues I always leave around the house for him to trip

Did Cinderella make things easy for the Prince by giving him her address or even her name?

over: A sales flier with a dog-eared corner. A catalog with a star next to an item on page seventeen. A casual comment flung into the room during the fourth quarter of the Super Bowl game.

And *he* asks how he's supposed to know.

The nerve.

Yes, men are supposed to read our minds. When it comes to fights, presents—and especially when it comes to romance—our husbands would do well to don swami turbans and read crystal balls. They might as well, you know, because it is certainly unreasonable to expect us to make things easy for them by actually *verbalizing* the things that we want and need.

After all, did Cinderella make things easy for the Prince by giving him her address or even—heaven forbid!—her name? Of course not.

Did Sleeping Beauty leave written instructions by the side of the bed: "To awaken Princess, kiss once"? No way.

Did Juliet alert Romeo to the fact that the poison she consumed was, indeed, temporary and that he was supposed to cool his heels and wait for her to regain consciousness so they could live together forever? Not a chance.

When it comes to romance, men are supposed to "just know" when to call, when to kiss, and when to give us a little space to come to our senses.

I'll admit, it's a flawed system. But it's a time-honored system that has been around a lot of years.

Bedroom Telepathy

Correct me here if you think I'm going too far with this, but sometimes I wonder if this system accounts for some of the misunderstandings that can occur in the bedroom. I know that, personally, I'd love for my husband to magically ascertain and then respond to all of my unspoken sexual needs. I want him to *just know* when to kiss me, how to hold me, what to say and do in the bedroom to drive me wild with passion.

I don't want to have to tell him these things.

Recently I've been interviewing women about this very subject. What I want to know is this: Am I the only woman who tries to communicate telepathically with her husband about sex?

Apparently not.

Carrie is a newlywed, married for a little over a year. She says that during lovemaking she doesn't mind expressing her feelings about things that she enjoys. She will tell her husband, "I like this or that . . ." or "I would enjoy it if you would . . ." On the other hand, she hesitates to let him know when he initiates something that she doesn't like. As a result, there are times during lovemaking when she feels turned-off.

Paula, married seventeen years, is the mother of three. Her story is the reverse of Carrie's. Paula says she "definitely" tells her husband when something about their lovemaking makes her uncomfortable. But when there is something new she would like to try, Paula "feels funny" speaking up. Instead, she keeps silent or tries to find non-verbal methods of communicating her desires.

Ann has been married eleven years. She feels comfortable telling her husband what she likes—and doesn't like—about sex. What is difficult for her to do, however, is initiate sex. One night she was so frustrated with her inability to communicate her desires to her husband—and so frustrated that he was lying right next to her and somehow not "picking up" on the fact that she wanted to make love—that she reached out her arm and, with one swipe, emptied her bedside table of all its contents. Digital clock, lamp, and books went flying. To the amazement of her husband, Ann went downstairs and spent the night on the couch. She says she realized even then that she was overreacting, but she felt trapped—trapped by her own silence, and trapped by the belief that somehow her husband should have had the power to sense her dilemma and rescue her from that silence.

I don't want to suggest that sex with our husbands should epitomize all of our secret desires and fantasies, or that we have a right to demand the fulfillment of our every sexual whim, or that lovemaking should be engineered to meet our needs and our needs only.

After all, a marriage license doesn't guarantee that our every sexual desire, need, or whim will be fulfilled. It does, however, give us the legitimate, God-ordained opportunity to *seek the fulfillment* of those desires, needs, and even whims. Marriage creates the possibility—even the probability—of having those desires met. But in order for this to happen, we need to be able to take the plunge and be willing to ask for what we need in the bedroom.

Four Myths about Men, Women, and Sex

I believe there are four myths that discourage many women from being more verbal about their sexual needs and desires. No one may have actually verbalized these words to you or to me, but the concepts—almost by osmosis—seem to have seeped into the collective subconsciousness of women everywhere. They hinder many of us from being more honest in the bedroom and help foster our expectations that our men can and should know instinctively—with little help from us—how to meet our needs and desires. Ready? Here they are:

Myth #1: Men Are Omniscient

Sounds outrageous, doesn't it? Men? All-knowing? No way. After all, it took my husband three weeks to notice that I'd bleached my hair from brunette to blonde. Two months after I bought new wicker for the kitchen, Larry furrowed his brows at the chairs and asked, "Where did these come from?" But I can't be too harsh; we just passed our third year in this house and I think he knows where the silverware drawer is now. Good man . . . good provider . . . good father . . . but omniscient?

Wait. Hear me out. Think about our romantic icons. When it comes to heroes and heroines, the stories all sound pretty familiar. Men are the providers, the rescuers. They are the brawn *and* the brains. Throughout *Gone with the Wind,* who knew what Scarlett needed and wanted even when Scarlett herself was in the dark? Rhett, of course. Rhett knew how to handle Scarlett—knew how to talk to her, woo her, match wits with her, make love to her. Even when Rhett's actions exasperated Scarlett, we could see that he was making the right moves. We knew that, in the end, Scarlett would see that Rhett knew best all along.

In fairy tales, the knights and princes always seem to know who to rescue and how to go about it. But how do they know? Did Sleeping Beauty, Rapunzel, or even Snow White ever actually *ask* for help? Of course not. Yet somehow, some prince somewhere was alerted and rode to the rescue. And have you ever noticed that these guys don't have real names? Just The Prince. As if any prince will do. They're all clairvoyant, after all.

What about you and me? Are we still waiting for a psychic prince? If our husbands rode white steeds into our bedrooms—suddenly transformed into omniscient heroes who knew what we needed without our having to tell them—would any of us be too disappointed? Okay, I'll admit, horse apples on the carpet would be a slight drawback, but other than that, I think I could be pretty happy with the arrangement. My guess is that you could too.

Myth #2: Boys Will Be Boys

There is a flip side to the perception of men as omniscient, and it is the perception that men don't have the maturity to handle certain facts about sex.

Carrie—the newlywed who admitted that she never tells her husband when something about their lovemaking turns her off—says that she is afraid speaking out would hurt his feelings, even wound his ego.

Another friend shrugs her shoulders when she talks about her husband's "inability" to help her transition into sex. She says her husband's idea of foreplay is the thirty seconds it takes to lock the bedroom door so the kids don't barge into the room. She admits this approach doesn't do much for her, but she justifies his behavior by saying, "Men are just like that."

Are we, by our silence, trying to protect the men we love—men we perceive as being too fragile or immature to handle the things we want, and need, to say? If so, we might be successful for a while. But as the years of marriage add up, we run the risk of building resentment

One woman said her husband's idea of foreplay was the time it took to lock the bedroom door.

toward the men whose egos we fought so hard to protect, while our needs go virtually unnoticed. Even worse, if we perceive our husbands as being too immature to consider any sexual needs but their own, we run the risk of losing respect for our spouses. Either emotion—resentment or disdain—is bound to seep beyond the bedroom door and poison our marriages.

Myth #3: Women Don't Have Needs—Sexual or Otherwise

I'm quite certain you are familiar with this concept.

We are, after all, perceived as the nurturers and caregivers in our families, our churches, our communities. This is, for the most part, a wonderful thing and a privilege. Unfortunately, sometimes it feels like we're trapped in a role from which there is no escape. Sometimes it feels like being a woman, and especially being a mother, is little more than a succession of preemptions in which the needs of every other member of the human race—and I use the term "human" loosely here so as to include teenagers as well—take priority over our needs.

In life—and particularly in raising our children—it seems as though we aren't really allowed to have needs. And if a need does manage to creep in somewhere, isn't there a script somewhere in our minds that tells us it should be subjugated to the needs of other family members?

And what about in the bedroom? Does this philosophy apply even there? Are our sexual needs in some way secondary to those of our husbands'? Three out of three women I spoke with said yes. Okay, okay. I'll admit that three women does not a survey make, but take a moment and listen to their comments:

Newlywed Carrie agreed that her opinion might not be the "liberated, politically correct" thing to say, but she wanted to be honest. Yes, she thought her husband's sexual needs seemed more important than hers. After all, she said, statistically speaking, don't men think about sex more often than women do? Shouldn't that give them priority in the bedroom?

Another woman, the wife of a pastor, told a gathering of women that her main role in life is to meet her husband's sexual needs so that he doesn't become tempted when counseling lonely or hurting women in their congregation.

A third woman, the wife of a law student, spoke about one of her sexual needs—the need to have more time to "transition" into sex. She went on, however, to say that this is not something she discusses with her husband: "They say that, sexually, women are like Crock-Pots—we need time to warm up. But we don't always get that time, and it's easier not to have to ask for it. It's simpler just to go ahead with the program. It's just easier not to have to talk about it."

Which leads us to yet another myth that impacts the way we view ourselves and our sexuality.

Myth #4: Nice Women Don't Talk about Sex

I like sex. I've always liked sex. Before I married my husband, I had never actually experienced sex, but I knew even then that I was going to like it. The thing, however, that I couldn't do for a long time was talk about sex.

Ironic confession from a woman writing a book like this one, but it's true.

I remember, one afternoon, eating a hamburger with Larry at Burger King. We weren't married at the time, weren't even engaged, just dating, albeit fairly seriously.

We were talking about some friends of ours who were . . . well, sleeping together. We were surprised—disappointed even—at their choice. But what *really* surprised me was the words I heard from my boyfriend's mouth in the middle of Burger King that day.

He said . . . he *actually* said . . . *sexual intercourse.*

Just like that. In a full-bodied voice, not even a whisper.

"Dave told me he and Jenny had sexual intercourse."

He said this in the middle of a fast-food restaurant, without even blushing.

I was mortified.

I was nineteen years old, and I could say things like "all the way" or "they *did it*" or maybe, if I was feeling very outrageous, I might say that someone "had sex." But not *sexual intercourse.* And certainly not *other* words, words like . . . well, *penis.* Never, never, never. Even reading the direction pamphlet from my box of tampons was pretty embarrassing. And watching those douche commercials on TV—particularly in mixed company—was excruciating. There should be a law against a young woman having to sit in the same room with a boyfriend or father while learning about that "not so fresh feeling" for the first time. Although, come to think of it, there's probably no other way to learn about it. Until watching the commercial, it had never crossed my mind to verbalize those particular words to my mother or any other woman, and in my nearly four decades of living, I have never had anyone approach me with such a question.

Do nice women talk about things of a sexual nature? With the exception of the Massengill women (who seem nice enough, though I probably wouldn't invite any of them to lunch), the answer is questionable.

Oh, in real life we talk about sex, sometimes, around the edges of the topic, with our closest of friends. But in the minds of too many women lives this image of the

The truth is, nice women need sex too.

perfect spiritual woman. She's nice. She's godly. And she has never, not once, said the words *sexual intercourse* on purpose, out loud, over a Burger King Whopper and fries.

So there we have it. These seem to be our unspoken guidelines, although I'll have to admit they make a pretty sorry bunch of paradigms by which to live:

- Men are omniscient and don't need to be told about women's sexual needs.
- Men are fragile or immature and can't handle being told about women's sexual needs.
- Women aren't supposed to have sexual needs.
- And if we do happen to come down with a need or two—not unlike catching mono or the flu—we certainly aren't supposed to talk about it.

I'll admit that these concepts seem extreme, seen in black and white on the printed page. And yet I'd wager that every one of us, in some way, at some level, has been affected by several—if not all—of these illusions.

Dispelling the Myths

The truth is simple. The truth is that men are not omniscient. Many of them—my husband tells me he's included in these ranks—are tired of being left in the dark and would actually appreciate a suggestion or directive now and then.

Men are not as fragile or as hopelessly immature as we tend to think they are.

Nice women need sex too.

And finally, communication in the bedroom is key. We have to talk about sex. Communication is, after all, the number-one prevention against misunderstandings and long-term resentments.

Ah, but how to go about it!

Here are some suggestions that might come in handy as you seek to improve your communication and develop greater integrity and honesty regarding your sexual needs:

- *Communication can be verbal or nonverbal.* With some nonverbal direction during lovemaking, you may be able to communicate quite effectively with your husband. Try repositioning his hand or your bodies, perhaps with an affirmative comment such as "This is better."
- *Communication can be negative or positive.* When possible, frame your words positively, avoiding defense-raising phrases such as "I hate it when . . ." or "What really bugs me is . . ." or even "You always . . ." Instead, try to communicate the reverse

by using lead-ins such as "I really enjoy . . ." or "I prefer it when we . . ."

Still, there may be times you need to tell your husband about something you don't like, and the subtle approach is just not working. You may need to explain if a particular act or attitude makes you feel turned off or embarrassed. Again, concentrate on your feelings ("I don't enjoy . . ." or "This makes me feel . . .") rather than resorting to accusatory or demeaning shots at your husband.

- *Communication is a two-way street.* After expressing some of your needs to your husband, ask him what you might do to better meet his needs. In the give-and-take of two-way communication, your husband might be less defensive and more willing to listen. You may learn a few things as well.
- *Practice the art of negotiation.* More often than we like to admit, life is about compromise. If your husband enjoys the missionary position and you prefer sex on the stair-stepper, agree to find times to satisfy each desire. Share fantasies. Agree to wear that Elvira costume now and then, and don't be afraid to negotiate the fulfillment of a few of your fantasies in return.
- *Never withhold sex as a weapon or negotiating tool.* Sexual communion between husband and wife is the wellspring of the marriage relationship—it is, indeed, the intimate sacrament that makes marriage something more than a friendship or business partnership. If you express a need and find that your husband is having a difficult time grasping the significance of what you are asking, avoid the temptation to suggest cold showers for a month. Remember that the small wounds and unkindnesses that husbands and wives inflict on each other are not easily salved.

- *Good communication benefits you—and your husband too.* Go ahead. Ask for what you need. You'll benefit from the effort. But your husband will benefit too. If your sexual needs are given appropriate attention, who knows? You might enjoy sex more, want sex more often, or become less inhibited in sexual situations with your husband. Do you think your husband would enjoy these kinds of developments? Besides, let's be honest: Being able to turn a woman genuinely inside-out with pleasure—real pleasure, no faking here—is an esteem-booster for any man. Don't deny your husband the satisfaction of becoming the best possible lover to his wife. Ask for what you need. Do it for you. Do it for him.

Your Odds of Success

There is, of course, one small hitch in all of this. There is the possibility that you will express your needs to your husband and that he will listen carefully, process your heartfelt words, look at you sincerely and say, in so many words, "No way."

If this happens infrequently, so be it. As I mentioned before, the simple fact that we experience and express a particular desire does not mean we have some sort of inalienable right to have that desire satisfied by our husbands. As much as we lament the fact, our husbands are free agents. We can't *make* them do anything (as evidenced by the long list of uncompleted—even unattempted—"honey-do" projects that we create and maintain in vain for the men in our lives)!

A realistic expectation, then, might be that a portion of our requests would be met happily by our husbands; a majority of our requests would be satisfied through some form of negotiation and compromise; and that some of our requests might be turned down completely, leaving us to negotiate within ourselves for some form of closure or management of that issue.

I believe that following these suggestions is much healthier and much more effective than the alternative of NEVER ASKING, and as a result, NEVER RECEIVING at all.

Before you ask your husband for what you need, ask yourself a question: *What do I need?* Perhaps it is a different frequency of intimacy, or a better "bridge" into sexuality as it is expressed with your husband, or the fulfillment of a particular sexual dream or fantasy. Perhaps you need to negotiate the cessation or redirection of an act or behavior that leaves you feeling humiliated. Maybe it is simply that you prefer sex in the mornings, or that you'd really like to reminisce and spend an evening just "making out" in the backseat of the car!

It's okay to want things. And it's okay to talk about the things we want. There are, of course, no guarantees in life—no marriage or husband or "sex life" is without flaws. But we owe it to ourselves, and to the men we love, to manage our sexuality with honesty, integrity, and a willingness to share not just our bodies, but something that is far more intimate: the verbalization of our very dreams and desires and needs.

Beat the Bedroom Blues

By the time my marriage approached, I was ready. I had certainly watched enough romantic movies and read enough books that I anticipated the unseen terrain of the intimacies of married life like the face of a long-awaited old friend. There was little doubt in my mind; I was going to have the most passionate, romantic marriage ever. Our bedroom would be our sanctuary of love. A paradise of passion. A haven for hot, steamy sex.

And why stop at the bedroom? How about the hearth in front of the fireplace? The shower? The workbench in the garage? The kitchen counter? In my mind's eye, dinner would hardly ever be served on time. How could it be when the very sight of me peeling onions would be enough to drive my husband into a frenzy of passion?

Unfortunately, intimacy, whether of the flesh or of the emotions, never seems to ripen in real life with the fertile ease with which it thrives in our imaginations.

We have such dreamy notions, so many romance-novel expectations. Yet are any of us really ready for the infringement of reality on the carefully packaged fantasies of our youth? Are any of us prepared for the first hint of trouble in paradise? Steeled for the first emotional wound or rejection or insensitivity or misunderstanding between husband and wife as lovers?

We dream of romance. What we get instead is real life.

Bummer.

Perhaps, for Adam and Eve in the springtime of their garden days, emotional and sexual intimacy was the most natural thing in the world. Perhaps, before they met their tragic destiny as fallen beings, Adam and Eve laughed and loved without anything to complicate their physical and emotional fellowship. We know they were naked without shame. We know their marriage, unlike any other marriage in the history of the world, began fresh and unfettered by myths and memories from their past (Past? What past?). For Adam and Eve, for a heartbeat of time before the fall, intimacy, love, and lovemaking must have been as sweet and pure as the newborn air they breathed.

For the rest of us, it's hard work.

When Fact and Fantasy Don't Meet

For some unknown reason, there seems to exist for most of us a vast chasm between our fantasies and reality—a yawning canyon separating our expectations and our experiences.

Then again, maybe the reasons for this gargantuan rift aren't so mysterious after all. For one thing, the sermons from the pulpit of the media at which our society worships paint a pretty unrealistic portrait of sex. Lovemaking is always steamy and never troubled. Couples on TV and in movies have sex at a rate that even rabbits would be hard-pressed to emulate. Sex is always hot and

Real life is making love to a man who wears his black dress socks to bed.

always available. Orgasms fly fast and furious. Couples pant and sweat and groan and holler. Women have perfect bodies, and men are perfect lovers.

In the movies, no one ever has to go to the bathroom or adjust their diaphragm or stop making love long enough to work out a cramp in their leg (except maybe on *Seinfeld!*). No one is ever in the middle of a romantic evening when their kid comes down with an ear infection or the cat throws up. The phone never rings. No one ever gains twenty pounds or goes bald at thirty. And no one ever insists on making love with the lights out.

No, according to Hollywood, passion eclipses everything. Physical pain. Emotional crisis. Wars and chaos and even common sense—*especially* common sense. When those love juices get boiling, watch out. Nothing else matters. Nothing else is supposed to matter. The earth moves. The birds sing. The stars spin. Angels dance and fireworks soar.

On the other hand, there's real life.

Real life is making love to a man who wears his black dress socks to bed.

Real life is having to steady your voice in the middle of an orgasm and yell through a locked door to an impatient six-year-old whining in the hallway, "Mommy's. Resting. Right. Now. Jason."

Real life is the missionary position. Again.

Real life is making love without kissing because you have a cold and your nose is leaking like a faucet and your husband wants your body but not your germs.

Diana, a friend of mine, summed up the difference between fantasy and real life with the following lament. She explained: "You never fantasize about men who throw their dirty socks in the corner of the bedroom. No, you fantasize about a guy who shows up in a stretch limo carrying red roses and urging you to hurry because they're holding the plane for just the two of you. And then the fantasy ends and you do a load of laundry and reheat last night's spaghetti for your kids."

Real life. It's imperfect and flawed and very, very human.

But it's all we've got.

Great Sex Is Worth Fighting For

Have you ever noticed that real life offers much less—and at the same time, so much more—than any of us could possibly imagine and hope for? I don't know about you, but I never wanted much: only perfection. Perfection in my husband, in my children, in my career, in myself.

Hah.

Life has given me so much less than I expected.

And so much more.

Take child rearing for example. When I purchased my first mail-order changing table from Sears . . . bought that first baby-name book . . . listened for the first time to the fast-paced dubDUBdubDUBdubDUB of the tiny heartbeat in my womb . . . my mind swam with Norman Rockwell portraits of family life.

When reality hit, there was more chaos and challenge than I ever imagined. The first time my daughter Kaitlyn did something really annoying—she was about two and I think it was the time she gouged holes in my husband's prized Bose speakers with a fork—I remember looking around and thinking to myself, "Now where's that manual? She *must* have come with some sort of a manual. . . ."

But there is no manual, is there? And no easy solutions. Parenting is hard work that takes us daily to the very limit of our mental, emotional, physical, and spiritual resources.

And yet the rewards! The rewards are so much greater than I ever could have imagined. When Kaitlyn was six, I measured the diameter of her face. Four inches. I was amazed. Just four inches of face. To imagine that of all the sights and sounds and mass and tangible objects in this entire universe, one of the greatest joys I had ever experienced could be evoked by simply catching a glimpse of something a mere four inches wide!

The work is world-class.

The rewards are astronomical.

I believe the same thing can be said for our love lives.

It's a concept that, even as I write the words, I have a hard time accepting. We aren't supposed to have to work

Would our expectations about sex make a good script for Fantasy Island or even Mission: Impossible?

at sex. It's just supposed to be there, fully bloomed and perfect, like some sort of inalienable right implied, although not spelled out, in our Constitution.

Reality paints a different picture.

In her book *Hot Monogamy* (Dutton, 1994), Dr. Patricia Love writes: "Your bodies are complex and ever-changing, and it can take years to learn each other's rhythms. . . . Creating lasting passion with one person requires dedication, a willingness to compromise, and some tolerance for emotional discomfort."

Reality calls for years of dedication, compromise, discomfort.

In other words: work. Reconciling the rift between fantasy and reality takes nothing less than hard work.

Common Problems, Destructive Solutions

When our real-life experiences are different from our romantic expectations, how do we reconcile that difference? How do we bridge the gap so we don't live our lives in frustration or disillusionment?

Let me begin by telling you about three solutions that don't work. In fact, they are downright destructive. In these situations, it's even possible that the cure may actually be worse than the disease itself! Here they are:

Denial

You may remember Ann from the previous chapter. When we last saw her, she was flinging alarm clocks from her bedside table, unable to express her sexual desires to her husband. Ann and John found trouble in paradise from the word go. Both virgins when they married, she entered matrimony with visions of nonstop romance and steamy lovemaking. He kept getting hung up on teachings from his church and parents that sex was something from which to refrain—and above all not something to enjoy!

Ann's initial response to this dilemma was short lived. She initiated sex, dressed provocatively for bed, suggested new positions and games to try. Within a few years, Ann had given up completely. She was tired of making all the effort. She retreated into a shell of withdrawal and denial that, eleven years later, she found she could not abandon at will.

Ann and John's original dilemma was unfortunate, but not insurmountable. Tragically, Ann's response only managed to evade the problem and prolong the years of suffering before this couple began to truly confront the issues between them.

Unfortunately, the list of destructive responses to the bedroom blues could go on and on.

Divorce

Another woman—I'll call her Pamela—sought resolution to her blues through divorce. When Pamela married her high school sweetheart in 1963, she thought sex would always consist mainly of kissing and heavy petting. When her new husband abandoned both kissing and petting and opted for a pattern of intercourse without any foreplay at all, Pamela found that, for her, in reality sex was a painful experience.

The marriage ended three years later, during which time Pamela had never experienced orgasm and, indeed, had rarely enjoyed lovemaking with her husband. The hurdle they faced in the bedroom, along with hurdles in other arenas of their marriage, seemed insurmountable and brought the relationship to a grinding halt.

Infidelity

Still another woman, unhappily married for three years, found herself garnering attention from a handsome, older coworker with a reputation for seducing young women in his office. Looking back, she admits that she's not surprised she ended up sharing his bed: "My husband and I seemed so incompatible in the bedroom, and I was so lonely. I have no doubt my vulnerability at

> *We think everyone else enjoys wild passion while we spend Saturday nights replacing the baking soda in the refrigerator.*

that time could be read a mile away." While the sexual attention was better than what she had experienced at home, she knew this was not the way she wanted to live her life, and she soon ended the affair.

When reality and fantasy seem separated by a yawning chasm, how can we reconcile the differences? More importantly, how can we reconcile the differences in a healthy and constructive manner?

For every bedroom dilemma, there are dozens, if not hundreds, of potential responses. Unfortunately, it's often too easy to respond in a way that:

- ignores the problem
- prolongs the problem
- even complicates the problem

It's obvious that denial, divorce, and infidelity aren't ideal answers. But how can we make better choices?

When reality falls far short of fantasy and we find ourselves having to work—actually work!—to bring our expectations and our experiences into better alignment, how do we go about it?

Infuse a Little Reality into Your Fantasies

One of the first things we can do is examine our expectations about sex and marriage. Are they realistic? Do they represent real life or would they make a better script for *Fantasy Island* or maybe even *Mission: Impossible*?

Personally, it was hard for me to let go of some of my more unrealistic expectations about romance and sex. I wanted roses and diamonds and words and deeds that would sweep me off my feet. Several years into my marriage, I missed the excitement and romance of dating so much that I actually grieved the loss of what had been a very pleasurable part of my life. I didn't want a new person in my life—I wanted to recapture a sense of adventure and the unknown with the man I had married. I wanted to be surprised by romance. I wanted to experience again the thrill of a first date and first kiss—with a man I had known for five years and who had been my husband for three.

Not a particularly easy task.

The reality is that the stability of married love *is* different than the flickering, beckoning, head-spinning, pulse-quickening unknowns of courtship. Courtship is exciting and romantic because it thrives on the edge of disaster; it is so poignant because it coexists with the threat that, at any moment, it could all fall apart and be lost forever. To expect the lifelong commitment of marriage to evoke the excitement and adventure created by the fragility of courtship . . . well, as they say here in Texas, that dog just won't hunt.

A friend of mine, married for six years, has yet to catch on to the fact that married life is *supposed* to be different from courtship illusions. As a result, Jill fantasizes frequently about a former boyfriend, a man she almost married not long before she met the man who became her husband. Jill hasn't spoken to Tom for eight years—and yet she meets him daily in her imagination, which she fuels by countless questions beginning with the words, "What if . . ."

I agree with Jill that her marriage to her husband is fraught with weak places and could stand some improvement. If her relationship at home were stronger, perhaps she wouldn't feel so drawn to illicit thoughts about a man she used to love. At the same time, if she took the mental energies and imagination she is expending on her fantasies about Tom and invested them into her marriage instead, she might be surprised at the results.

But right now, that seems difficult for Jill to do. She is caught in the power of unrealistic images of the only perfect man in the world—a man who lives entirely in her mind. Jill admits that, should she happen to cross paths with Tom one day, the man-in-the-flesh would surely bear no resemblance to the image she has created in her mind. After eight years, her memories of Tom have been shaped and reshaped so often by her fantasies that, she admits, they have little in common with the real man. In fact, *any* real man.

Our imaginations are powerful tools that enrich our lives to no end. Yet, allowed to run rampant, they can easily create images and expectations that are far beyond the power of any individual or any relationship to fulfill.

I suggested to Jill that she create a list reflecting characteristics of the "real" Tom—the one who walks in flesh and blood, not in her mind. The real Tom has morning breath. He takes too long in the bathroom. He never puts his dirty clothes in the hamper; it's entirely possible he has never even *seen* the hamper. He makes good money, but he doesn't know how to balance the checkbook. He always wants to make love with the overhead light on. He can burp on demand, which he does frequently to the delight of his children and the chagrin of his wife. He's losing his hair.

I suggested that she review this list every day. What a healthier, more realistic image for Jill's husband to compete against! And whether he realizes it or not, he *is* in competition.

All our husbands are. They're running a race against imaginary men who never forget an anniversary and imaginary marriages that even Donna Reed would envy. And it's just not fair.

In a sense, we've been deceived. As a nation, we've been duped into believing that when it comes to relationships, the grass is always greener on the other side. Other spouses are more romantic than ours. If we divorced our husbands and married other men, our lives might be better. No other couple faces the same struggles we do. The rest of the world is enjoying romance and wild passion while we're spending Saturday night replacing the baking soda in the refrigerator.

The realities are these: There are no perfect men. No perfect marriages. No perfect love lives. So let's stop pretending that there are. Until we do, until our expectations come down out of the stars and start hovering a little closer to ground level, we may never have a real shot at contentment and happiness with what we've got—real life.

Infuse a Little Fantasy into Your Reality

While we're bringing our *expectations* closer to ground level, how about encouraging our real-life *experiences* to leap and fly a little now and then? It's possible that by enhancing our reality with a little fantasy and at the same time working to infuse our fantasies with a little reality, we just might find some middle ground that can sustain a healthy marriage relationship over the years.

Make an investment in your love life. Don't assume that spark and sizzle occur naturally, or that it is somehow solely your husband's responsibility to bring romance and vitality back into your bedroom.

What do *you* want? Do you have specific thoughts, ideas, fantasies about what might enhance romance and lovemaking with your husband? If you do, then how might you begin today to implement some of those ideas?

If you aren't sure, if you just know that reality isn't measuring up and you aren't quite sure what to do about it, then experiment. Try something—ANYTHING—new and different. See what works and what doesn't.

Here's an idea. Put aside the flannel nightshirt for one night and wear something else. Anything else. Lingerie will work, but how about something *really* unexpected? Consider a trench coat a la carte. Or your Sunday best over a garter belt and stockings. Or wear nothing but one of your husband's ties.

Even uniforms can be sexy. I recently met a woman whose husband is on the police force of the town in which I live. She admitted to me that she has, on occasion, donned her husband's police uniform shirt, complete with badge and hat, to lend some pizzazz to their lovemaking. She says it's fun to role-play and that she and her husband laugh most of the way through the spicy encounters.

New dress, new places, new bedroom lighting—even small changes can reap significant rewards. Be creative. Have fun. Make the most of what you have to work with. Make reality count.

Celebrate Your Sexuality

Last week we celebrated Kaitlyn's birthday. She turned eight.

A week before the party I called around and found a skating rink that would provide a party—complete with ice cream, cake, party favors, balloons, and, of course, roller skating—for twenty kids for about a hundred bucks.

I was already writing invitations when I mentioned the plan to my husband.

He gasped. "A hundred dollars! Karen, that's ridiculous. We can give a party right here for a lot less."

I told him I agreed—in theory. Maybe I could do it for twenty-five dollars less. Or maybe even fifty dollars. What I didn't want to spend, however, was time and energy. I reminded him that I had a book deadline to consider. I reminded him that I was five months pregnant and that my body had, apparently, not been paying attention while I read all those pamphlets that assured me nausea and exhaustion go away after month number three. I reminded him that November in Texas meant we ran the chance of rain and hosting twenty eight-year-olds in the house.

He promised he would help.

The night before the party a thunderstorm blew in. The morning of our celebration, I looked out the window and saw a translucent blue sky windswept of every single cloud.

I should have been warned. We had used up all our luck on the weather.

The children arrived in energetic form. The boys migrated toward the playhouse at the back of our property; the girls congregated on the back porch for crafts.

Half an hour into the party, I was in the kitchen pouring punch when a gaggle of girls ran giggling through the kitchen and toward the front door. I stopped them. "Where are you going?"

Kaitlyn beamed. "Mark just climbed over the fence!"

I had a sudden vision of one of our young party goers leaving the celebration in an ambulance. I had a second

Celebrations take time and energy, but the memories we create are worth the effort.

vision of my little family huddled in the unemployment line since Mark is the son of the president of the university where my husband is employed.

I groaned and hurried out the front door with the girls.

Mark was ambling up the stairs to the front porch, wearing a face-splitting grin. The girls surrounded him, chattering wildly. The grin grew. He was a hero.

I got everyone safely returned to the backyard and looked around for my husband.

He was nowhere to be seen.

I went to the foot of the stairs and yelled up toward the bedrooms. "Larry?"

His answer came muffled through our closed (and probably barricaded) bedroom door.

"Where are you? It's time for the baseball game!"

He hurried down and rounded up the kids for baseball.

Twenty minutes later, the game over, I was in the kitchen slicing ice-cream cake when the posse of girls surrounded me again, breathless, excited. I asked, "What is it this time?"

"The boys are tearing the roof off the playhouse!" Kaitlyn beamed.

I went to the foot of the stairs. "Larry!"

"What?"

"I need you!"

He hurried down the stairs, out the back door, and soon had the kids rounded up for cake.

I guess there was just one other harrowing moment. That was when I glanced into the living room and saw my floral couch being lifted into the air. Okay, maybe it wasn't the whole couch—just the cushions. Larry herded the small ruffians into the kitchen in time to save the coffee table.

That night I was adding up the cost of our inexpensive little backyard party. Let's see: Cups. Plates. Ice-cream cake. Party favors. Craft and game supplies. Face paint. Balloons. My subtotal came to seventy-two dollars.

I was about to add eighty-five dollars in repairs to the playhouse and a thirty-dollar prescription of Valium for me when Kaitlyn came up and flung her arms around my neck.

"Mom, thanks for my party," she gushed. "It was so much fun! I liked it SO MUCH better than skating."

I threw away my ledger. I guess we had come out ahead after all.

Celebrating New Frontiers

We love to celebrate, don't we? Anniversaries. Birthdays. Holidays. We love picnicking in the summer and carving pumpkins in the fall and drinking cider by a roaring fire when the weather turns downright cold.

Celebrations take planning and energy, but somewhere deep inside we know that the memories we create when we celebrate are worth all the effort.

What are the components of celebration? When we celebrate something, we remember it, make time for it, show gratitude for it. We don't take it for granted. Sometimes we give it a special day. We have fun with it. We thank God for it.

What would happen if we applied the same attitude, planning, and energy to our love lives? What would happen if we didn't simply express our sexuality, but took the whole matter a step further and actually *celebrated* this incredible gift that we have been granted by our Creator?

Celebrate Your Sexuality by Planning Ahead

What could a little planning do to our love lives?

Ask Diane and Doug.

By the time their third child was born, Diane and Doug just didn't seem to have much time and energy left over for sex. For the first time in their lives, making love became something they happened to stumble into now and then, whenever circumstances were such that none of the kids had a fever and that at least one of the adults had gotten eight hours of sleep the night before.

That's when Diane and Doug made a commitment to each other, a commitment that could not be executed without considerable long-term planning. They decided to get away to a hotel for a long weekend once every three months.

That commitment has held for years. Sometimes the time stretches to six months between get-away weekends, but never longer than that. During their time away, Diane and Doug sleep late and eat out at nice restaurants. They take long walks together. They make love leisurely and without threat of interruption! They talk about their dreams and plans, and they spend time praying for each of their children.

I'll admit, entire weekends require *a lot* of planning. I also believe they are worth the effort and the expense. It's possible, however, that you might want a little practice at planning before working up to something as grand as an entire weekend. If so, how about setting aside a single day in which to plan ahead for sex?

Jennifer Louden, in her user-friendly manual entitled *The Couple's Comfort Book* (HarperCollins, 1993), outlines an exercise in anticipation that she calls "Simmering Sexual Feelings." Sounds like a recipe, I know. And, in many respects, it is—a recipe for renewed passion for two. Louden suggests beginning the day in the following manner:

> Roll over and caress your mate while whispering in his or her ear, "I want to make love to you tonight like lions mating on the veld." (Or something like that.) Don't squelch this by saying, "But tonight's the PTA meeting."

> If tonight isn't a good time for you, then lick your lover's ear and gently propose an alternative date.
>
> Throughout the day, massage your anticipation. Make whispered illicit phone calls about what you are going to do to each other that night; have lingerie, silk boxer shorts, scented massage oil, or a canister of whipped cream delivered to work with a naughty note. . . . Spend the day simmering your excitement. . . .
>
> Once together in the evening, keep building the tension. Rub against each other "accidentally" while you're cooking dinner, go out to dinner together and feed each other, take a shower together, take time to arrange the atmosphere in your bedroom, and then, finally, time for love. (Yes, you can do this with children. Five minutes of sexual innuendo over dessert while the kids watch TV, ten minutes of foreplay while the kids are in the bath, fifteen minutes of intercourse after the kids fall asleep. Be creative; it doesn't have to be one continuous encounter!)

Go ahead. You can admit it and I won't tell a soul. It sounds like fun, doesn't it?

By advocating planning, I don't want to discredit the value of spontaneity. It's just that, in our busy lives, spur-of-the-moment opportunities to create lasting memories together are rare and golden. Planning ahead assures that

Planning ahead lets your husband know how much you value time together.

these moments won't be overlooked entirely in the hustle and bustle of our daily lives. Planning ahead also lets your spouse know how much you value your times together.

In the month or two after our first baby was born, sex just didn't seem like a high priority to me. I was sore, I was exhausted, and I was completely emotionally sated by the new love in our lives. I was also just weeks removed from the trenches of childbirth and wasn't too keen on doing anything that might reenlist me for a second tour of duty.

Still, in some buried part of my psyche I knew that sex remained important—for my husband, and for me as well.

I called Biola University where my husband was, at that time, chairman of the business department. I got Larry's secretary on the phone and asked her to set up a lunch appointment for Larry with an imaginary prospective student and his parents. Then I asked her to block out the rest of his afternoon. I arranged for a babysitter, then phoned a local motel down the street and reserved a room, which I stocked with flowers, grapes, a bottle of sparkling apple cider, and even our swimsuits in case we felt like hitting the pool.

On the appointed day I picked up Larry at his office and told him—surprise!—that I was his real lunch date. I then drove him to a Chinese restaurant that just happened to be on the first floor of the motel I had chosen. After we ordered, I suggested taking a walk around the motel gardens until our food arrived. On our way out, I slipped a note to our waiter asking for lunch to be delivered to our room. Outside, I placed a room key in Larry's hand and then waited for him to pick his jaw up off the sidewalk.

No interruptions. No baby crying. No rush, which was important to me since I was still wary about making love for the first time after the rigors of childbirth. Our Chinese food was cold by the time we retrieved it from outside the door, and we never did make it to the pool. It cost me eighty bucks and took a week to plan.

But what a celebration.

Celebrate Your Sexuality by Trying New Things

Surprise. Isn't that the element that makes courtship so enticing? Before I married, how I loved to be surprised by romance! A first kiss, a bouquet of flowers, a romantic card, the first words of commitment from someone I cared about, a long-awaited proposal, an engagement ring hidden in a box of Cracker Jack! I'm married now, and guess what? I still like surprises!

There is a place for predictability. I certainly wouldn't want my life to resemble a roller coaster all the time! But now and again it certainly doesn't hurt to have things shaken up a bit by the new and unexpected.

Particularly in the area of marital romance.

What would happen if you made a point to try something new, let's say, oh . . . once a month? The possibilities range from the subtle to the outrageous; all it takes is a little imagination.

It might be as simple as surprising your husband by donning new lingerie and making love by the light of several dozen candles. One author I read suggested beginning with new lingerie and candles, and then adding the following: a few "tropical-looking" plants for your bedroom, a fake animal throw for the bed, a musky-scented candle or other room fragrance, and some sort of primitive, tribal-sounding music.

One woman I know told me that she sat in a chair and allowed her husband to blindfold her loosely. This was not an exercise in sexual bondage, but rather in vulnerability and trust. Her sight restricted, she found her other senses heightened as her husband ministered to her with gentle kisses and caresses. After a few moments, they traded places. Remembering the experience later, she says she and her husband had never tried anything similar in nearly twenty years of marriage, but that the moment—coming after a time of emotional estrangement and recommitment in her marriage—was one of great tenderness and rediscovery for her and her husband.

A few years ago my husband and I decided to try something we had never done before. Driving in the car, we decided to find a secluded place for love. Now, in my dating days I had certainly steamed up the windows in a car or two, but the intimacy in which I engaged had always been circumvented by strict boundaries. I had never attempted anything like what we were about to try.

The difficult part was finding a secluded place to park. We must have driven for half an hour. I told my husband this was ridiculous—high school kids found these kinds of places every Friday and Saturday night, and here two

Adventure is great, but there's a lot to be said for familiarity and comfort as well.

intelligent, college-educated adults couldn't find a darkened parking lot to save their lives. We laughed throughout the experience. It's the kind of thing that, afterward, you describe as "interesting." All in all, I'm glad I'm a thirty-something married woman with one kid and another on the way, a dog, a cat, and a mortgage—and my own bedroom to share with a committed husband. But it was something new and, even if it's not repeated in the near future, it added a dose of adventure and fun to our love life!

When trying new things, there is one rule, and it is a condition that you may want to discuss beforehand with your husband. It's one thing to laugh *with* your spouse. It's quite another to laugh *at* your spouse. Years after the fact, one of my friends still speaks with a note of hurt and rejection in her voice when she recalls the time she tried to surprise her husband by dressing up and trying to "act sexy" not unlike the characters in movies or on TV. Her husband laughed at her efforts, and she bears the scars of his teasing to this day.

Celebrate Your Sexuality with Familiar Rituals

We can celebrate by planning. We can celebrate by trying something new. We can also celebrate our sexuality by creating lasting memories through familiar rituals.

When something meaningful is repeated and reenacted through the years, it becomes more than a memory, even more than a tradition. It becomes part of the fabric of your life. It begins to shape who you are. And if you share the tradition with someone you love, it can shape and enrich that relationship as well.

When it comes to sexuality, familiar rituals become something special shared by just the two of you. It strengthens an emotional bond. Occasionally it can also allow you to experience intimacy with very little investment or risk. On a given night you may be too tired to invest a lot of emotional energy in a sexual encounter; a familiar ritual allows you to relax and follow an established pattern. Familiar rituals can provide a sense of safety and comfort.

Here are a few examples: One woman I know lights a scented candle in the bedroom whenever she wants to let her husband know she's feeling amorous. Another woman says that Friday night after the kids are asleep has evolved into a weekly date with her spouse. This two-career couple knows that during these evenings they don't have to be creative or take a long time—this is a familiar way of reconnecting with each other after the week-long flurry of living virtually separate lives. Finally, a third friend says she and her husband end every birthday—

hers and his—by sneaking some leftover cake into their bedroom at night and feeding it to each other in bed.

A familiar ritual doesn't even have to culminate in intercourse. On evenings when you and your husband are getting dressed to go out, you might develop the habit of offering to help him with his tie and sharing a kiss while your arms are around his neck.

During my childhood, whenever my family was traveling in the car and my dad asked for a piece of gum, my mother always unwrapped the gum for him and sweetened it with a kiss before handing it over.

In the months after Kaitlyn was born and I found myself crawling in and out of bed numerous times each night to breastfeed, my husband began a small ritual that meant a lot to me in those predawn hours. A sound sleeper, he rarely woke completely as the baby cried and I crawled out of and, much later, back into bed. But each time I returned to the sheets, he reached an arm behind him, found whatever part of my anatomy was nearby, and gave me a warm pat. Two, three, even six times a night, he acknowledged my efforts with the gentle gesture. It was just enough to say, "I know what you're doing. I know you're having to get up and down. I know you're making a sacrifice."

There's something to be said for excitement and adventure. But there's an awful lot to be said for familiarity and comfort as well. By finding small ways to share your affection and celebrate your sexuality—and repeating them through the years—they will soon take on the rich patina that only a lifetime of loving can impart.

A Biblical Celebration of Married Love

There is something I am going to ask you to do.

Whenever I'm reading a book and the author asks me to do something that takes me outside of the pages I'm holding, well . . . I fudge. I pretend I did whatever it was he or she asked for, and I skip right on to the rest of the text.

Assure me you won't do that, and I promise to make this quick.

Right now, put this book down and walk to your library or den bookshelves or to the quiet place where you have devotions and retrieve your Bible.

Now's fine.

Don't fudge.

Go ahead. I'll wait.

* * * * * * * * * * *

Thanks. Now turn to the Song of Songs. Past Psalms, Proverbs, Ecclesiastes . . . There it is. Short, isn't it? Six pages in all. It won't take five or ten minutes, but I'd like you to read those pages. They provide a fitting close to this chapter on celebration of sexuality, and they will also prepare you for the following chapter, which is on developing a biblical perspective on sexuality.

The six pages you are about to read describe nothing less than a celebration extraordinaire of sexual love and desire. Our sexuality, expressed and protected in the context of a loving marriage, is a gift from God. As such, we have every right and reason to remember it, make time for it, have fun with it, and thank God for it.

Now take a few minutes and read what Solomon—the wisest man in the world—had to say about making love to the wife that he adored, and see if these two folks didn't have a handle on celebrating their sexuality!

Go ahead. I'll catch up with you in the next chapter.

Develop a Biblical Perspective on Sex and Sexuality

When one friend learned that I was writing an ABC book on sexuality for women—and that my goal was for this book to be lighthearted, user-friendly, and fun in addition to being factual and biblically sound—she practically clapped her hands in glee. "I love the idea!" she said, adding, "It certainly needs to be written. Just imagine how glad readers will be to learn that they can be Christians and love sex too!"

I share her tongue-in-cheek perspective. I, too, continue to be amazed by people—some who profess to be religious and others who do not—who have come to the misbegotten conclusion that in the eyes of God, sex is somehow dirty or wrong.

Of course, the complete opposite is true. In fact, Scripture gives us a veritable banquet of commands, suggestions, and images related to God's high opinion of the sensual pleasures available to husbands and wives! It's true. It's really true! We can be Christians—we can love and obey and seek to glorify God with our lives—and we can love sex too. There is no conflict. In fact, when we actively enjoy sensual pleasures with our husbands, we are pleasing and actually obeying God.

Our Sexuality Was Not a Divine Blooper

I never actually saw the movie *The Blue Lagoon,* but I understand that it was about a young man and woman stranded together on a beautiful island. The message of the movie producers seemed to be this: In the midst of beauty and isolation, the sexual awakening of these two young people was not only pure and natural, but entirely unavoidable.

What do you think was in God's mind as he created two human beings, a man and a woman, and placed them—stark naked!—to live alone and isolated in the most beautiful setting on the face of the earth? Was he surprised at the sexual awakening of these two physically flawless beings he had created one for another? Did he see the way their bodies knit and moved together during lovemaking and muse to himself, "Now look at what they've gone and done. I certainly didn't have *that* in mind when I gave Adam that there appendage and created those nooks and crannies for Eve."

If moviegoers were not surprised by the sexual discoveries made by two fictional characters on a deserted island, I'll wager that God was not surprised when he created Adam and Eve with complementary physical equipment and placed them in a romantic and isolated setting. In fact, I believe he knew precisely what he was doing.

In the first few pages of their book *The Act of Marriage* (Zondervan, 1976), Tim and Beverly LaHaye set out to show that not one but all three members of the Trinity have—in some way or other—given their "stamp of approval" on sex between husband and wife.

Their first example is taken from the garden scene when God, in Genesis 1:28, commands Adam and Eve to "be fruitful, and multiply, and replenish the earth" (KJV). The LaHayes point out that this "charge was given before sin entered the world; therefore, lovemaking and procreation were ordained and enjoyed while man continued in his original state of innocence." In other words, married love was part of God's perfect plan; sex was not something that "snuck" into the picture as a result of sin. It is not, like divorce, something that God allows but that is not his perfect will for our lives.

Secondly, the LaHayes observe that the Lord Jesus Christ chose a wedding as the event at which to perform his first miracle—something he would not have done if weddings, and the pending sexual intimacy they imply, were somehow less than God's perfect plan for us. Then

There is nothing spiritual about a marriage in which sex is ignored or repressed.

later, in Matthew 19:5, Jesus describes marriage not in terms of the ceremony, but as the moment when a man is "joined to his wife, and the two shall become one flesh." What a beautiful description of lovemaking between husband and wife!

Finally, the Holy Spirit inspired the writer of Hebrews to record this principle: "Marriage is honorable among all, and the bed undefiled" (Hebrews 13:4). And perhaps, if we are looking for God's stamp of approval on marriage and all that it entails, we needn't look any further than Proverbs 18:22, where Solomon, also under the inspiration of the Holy Spirit, writes simply: "He who finds a wife finds a good thing, and obtains favor from the Lord."

What do these verses tell us?

They remind us that the male/female differences in our bodies—the unique way that they complement each other and fit together during lovemaking—are not an accident, but were designed intentionally by God.

They also remind us that God is not in the dark about sexuality in marriage. He is not only aware, but he is in approval of this wonderful experience for husbands and wives.

Sexuality Is Not Just for Procreation

I remember when I was ready to . . . well, procreate. I was twenty-six and my husband and I had been married for five years. Before venturing into parenthood, we had wanted to accomplish a few things: Larry wanted to finish his doctorate. I wanted to finish my bachelor's degree. Finally, we wanted to save some money for a down payment on a house.

We had purchased our first little house and were still living out of boxes when I figured the prerequisites had been satisfied. I told Larry I thought we were ready for a baby.

He said he'd like to enjoy a few more months without the pending threat of having to carry a diaper bag and childproof all the bathroom cabinets.

I told him I was twenty-six and that my eggs were aging even as we spoke.

He suggested that waiting a few months would give us a little extra time as a two-income family.

I told him it could take months and months for me to get pregnant, and that we should start trying now.

He said he'd heard of women getting pregnant right away.

I told him we could compromise. I suggested using birth control one night, going without for the next, in alternating fashion. I told him to think of it as a game. Like Russian roulette.

Naturally I got pregnant the first night. Of course, we *had* been practicing for five years—as we should have been. It's true that sex is God's way of bringing babies into our world and continuing the generations. But it's also true that God designed sex to fulfill a number of other purposes in the marriage relationship. Let me tell you about three of them.

Sex Is Designed for Fun

A woman I know named Peggy says that while she was growing up, her mother made it clear that sex was *not* supposed to be fun. Mom was, in fact, explicit in her instructions to her daughters that sex was for procreation. Aside from that, well, it was something a woman had to put up with now and then.

As a society we've come a long way from those philosophies. Peggy, now an adult and a mother herself, is one of the first to admit that God designed sex for our enjoyment: "It took me a few years to understand the role that God had intended sexuality to play in our marriage. I'm grateful that both God and my husband had patience with my learning curve! Now, I can honestly say that the playfulness and enjoyment that takes place in our bedroom is one of the reasons our marriage has lasted for twenty-one years."

Of course, it's highly possible that Peggy could find a happy moment during a root canal; she is an upbeat, energetic woman whose smile is as sincere as it is perpetual. But I don't think she's exaggerating when she talks

God makes it clear that husbands and wives should satisfy each other.

about the joyous celebration of sexuality between a husband and wife. And she's right.

King Solomon—known far and wide for his exceptional wisdom—instructed his son to "rejoice with the wife of your youth. . . . [and] let her breasts satisfy you at all times; and always be enraptured with her love," (Proverbs 5:18–19).

I don't know about you, but in my opinion these words have nothing to do with procreation or with duty. This is meant for *fun*. Pay close attention to Solomon's choice of words: Rejoice. Satisfy. Be enraptured.

After the last chapter, you took a few moments to read the story of Solomon's love affair with a woman who was his fiancée and, eventually, his bride. Before their wedding, the couple speaks in poetic and sometimes veiled language regarding the sexual passion they feel toward one another; after the wedding, that passion is finally satisfied in each others' arms. Once again, a picture is painted of the sheer beauty and rapture of the physical passion shared by husband and wife.

For example, he praises her eyes and hair and smile and breasts, then adds: "You have ravished my heart with one look of your eyes."

She describes him to her friends as handsome and pleasant, then adds: "Like an apple tree among the trees of the woods, so is my beloved among the sons. I sat down in his shade with great delight, and his fruit was sweet to my taste."

He says the curves of her thighs are like jewels, her breasts are like clusters of grapes, her breath is like the fragrance of apples and the roof of her mouth is like the best wine.

She says, "I am my beloved's, and his desire is toward me."

Wouldn't it be wonderful if this God-given image of married love could be projected—like a hologram blueprint!—onto your marriage and mine as well? This is the picture of what God wants for your marriage. Don't let anyone convince you otherwise.

Sex Is Designed to Protect Us from Dangers beyond Our Front Doors

Sexual expression outside the protective embrace of marriage is dangerous! Consider, for a moment, AIDS. Or unwanted pregnancies. Or the guilt and destruction of extramarital affairs. And as if these aren't enough to convince you . . . well, remember the movie *Fatal Attraction.* God makes it clear that, for reasons such as these, husbands and wives should satisfy each other and not deprive each other of the powerful experience of sexual love. In fact, through the apostle Paul God instructs husbands and wives to be intimate *frequently:*

> Nevertheless, because of sexual immorality, let each man have his own wife, and let each woman have her own husband. Let the husband render to his wife the affection due her, and likewise also the wife to her husband.

> The wife does not have authority over her own body, but the husband does. And likewise the husband does not have authority over his own body, but the wife does.
>
> Do not deprive each other except with consent for a time, that you may give yourselves to fasting and prayer; and come together again so that Satan does not tempt you because of your lack of self-control.
>
> 1 Corinthians 7:2–5

A firm foundation of sexual love in a marriage is one of the first and best defenses against the lures and dangers of an immoral world.

When I began attending Biola University fresh out of high school, I took a number of Bible survey courses from Dr. Curtis Mitchell. Dr. Mitchell was a legend on campus, having taught Old and New Testament courses to incoming students for umpteen years. He was known as a strict but fair grader and had won the respect of literally thousands of students through the decades. Above all, Dr. Mitchell brought a frank and fresh perspective to many of the passages we studied.

I remember being shocked, as a virginal college freshman, when Dr. Mitchell discussed some of the Bible's passages on sexuality. I remember the day he addressed the passage quoted above by saying, without so much as an apology or a blush, "Ladies, if a man has a Cadillac at home in the garage, there's no need for him to go down the street and drive a Volkswagen." There were, of course, equally frank admonitions for the young men in our class.

There is nothing spiritual or godly about a marriage in which sex is ignored or denied or repressed. Indeed, it is God's ideal plan for each of us to have available to us—and to make available to our husbands as well—Cadillacs or Jaguars or Mercedes, engines warm and idling, in our bedrooms.

Sex Is Designed for Intimacy

One woman admitted to me that "sex is the one thing I share with my husband that I share with him alone."

What a concept! And how true! Think about it. *Every other arena or activity in marriage is subject to involvement by other people.* I cook for my husband, but I cook for other people too. We eat dinner together (most evenings), but I share meals with friends and colleagues and even strangers on a weekly basis. We raise our children together, but I could certainly enlist the help of a nanny if I was so inclined. What about other "duties" of marriage? We pay bills. Big deal. Hire an accountant. In fact, I can hire complete strangers to decorate my home, mow the lawn, repair the toilet, change the lightbulbs, deliver my groceries, listen to my problems, and—my personal favorite here—CLEAN MY HOUSE.

I can delegate all these things and still have a strong and healthy marriage.

What I can't do—and still have a marriage—is pay someone else to ring my chimes. Sexual intimacy is the one sacred event that my husband and I share with no one but each other: No hired hands allowed. Sexual intimacy is, indeed, the single dynamic that makes a marriage something more than a lifetime business partnership or a co-op between roommates.

There are, of course, couples for whom intercourse has been curtailed by illness or disability. I don't want to imply that these couples are living in anything less than a real marriage. For these couples, some form of physical intimacy—even if it has been modified by something beyond their control and even if it does not culminate in intercourse—can and should remain a viable part of the relationship.

What happens when a man and wife are emotionally and physically vulnerable with each other? There is a bond, a connection, that is absolutely imperative for couples living in today's fast-paced world of phones, faxes, and Federal Express. I know that for me sexual intimacy provides a feeling of oneness with my husband that lasts a good three days. After that, I find that I am much more susceptible to allowing the busyness of everyday life to drive wedges in our relationship.

Sexuality as a Spiritual Metaphor

The Bible is filled with word pictures that help us better understand the subtleties of our relationships with an intangible, invisible God. In fact, nearly every significant relationship in our lives can be used, in some way, to represent some great spiritual truth.

My relationship with my loving and nurturing earthly parents helps me to better understand my relationship with my loving and nurturing heavenly Father. I have two sisters, and my understanding of the rivalry, compassion, and camaraderie in sibling relationships prepares me better for the dynamics that can occur in my relationship with other believers, my brothers and sisters in Christ. Even my marriage can illustrate a spiritual truth to me; the Bible, after all, describes the church as the bride and Jesus Christ as her patient and loving bridegroom.

Then there are the natural drives that God has placed within each and every one of us: the need for food, water, shelter, sex. We hunger for *food,* and Jesus is called the Bread of Life. Our physical bodies thirst for *water,* and the Bible refers to this basic need to teach us that Jesus alone can give us Living Water so that we never spiritually thirst again. *Shelter?* God is portrayed as a fortress, the Holy Spirit uses you and me as his personal abode, and Jesus Christ has gone on to heaven to prepare a home for us for eternity.

Sometimes I wonder: What about sexuality? Sexuality is, after all, the foundation of the marriage relationship that God compares to Christ's relationship with the Church. In addition, the human need for sexual expression is also one of the driving forces that shape our very lives and many of our more profound choices. What spiritual truths could possibly be mirrored in the dynamic of our sexuality?

Sex is the foundation of marriage, which God uses to illustrate Christ's relationship with the church.

Now don't go quoting me on this—I am not, after all, a theologian—but let me share with you a few thoughts I've had on this matter.

There is something in the intimate, fertile, loving bond between a husband and wife that seems to speak to me of the saving work of Jesus Christ, and also of the regenerative work of the Holy Spirit in our lives as believers.

Think about it for a moment. Beginning with salvation, what is required of us? Nothing, except for explicit trust and vulnerability. All that is required is that we stand, honest and naked, with all of our flaws and imperfections glaring, before a loving God who accepts us as we are and who desires, through our union with him, to bring new life and love and vitality into our lives. When we accept Christ, the Holy Spirit enters us, and thus begins an intimate relationship with God that is life-giving and powerful. This relationship, this level of intimacy with our

Creator, changes us, transforms us as only the deepest kind of love can do. It births in us new desires, new thoughts, and new images of the kind of men and women God desires for us to become.

Too many women and men hold God at arm's length. Yes, they are "born-again." Yes, they believe in salvation through the spilled blood of Jesus Christ. Yes, they intellectually embrace what the Bible has to say. But when it comes to real intimacy—to heartfelt worship, to the deepest levels of vulnerability and transparency in their prayer life, to vulnerability and transparency with other believers, to total submission to the work of the Holy Spirit in their lives, to absolute yielding of private stashes of sin and rebellion—well, that kind of intimacy is too uncomfortable. Too embarrassing. Too personal. How much simpler to settle for a barren, platonic friendship with God! It doesn't bear much fruit, but it sure is comfortable.

We all live with the temptation to allow our relationships with God—and our relationships with our husbands as well—to stagnate into the kind of sterile partnership I've described above. But there's something better, isn't there? And it's intimate and fertile and life changing. It requires effort and transparency and risk.

But it's worth it.

Embrace the Art of Sensuality

I just got off the phone with a friend named Bonnie. As a realtor, she is constantly in her car, driving to homes, meeting clients, delivering documents. Go, go, go. Today she admitted that on this particular dark and rainy afternoon there's nothing she'd like more than to stay indoors in the glow of a roaring fire and spend an intimate hour or two with her husband. It's a classic scene of romance that holds a common fascination for all of us, isn't it?

And why shouldn't it? Such a scene is more than sexual. It's *sensual.* It appeals to all the five senses. Think about it: the crackle of the logs in the fireplace, the smell of woodsmoke curling languidly into the chimney, the heat of the fire warming our bodies. The visual contrast of the bright, hypnotic flames casting about in a darkened room. The fire's glow reflected in the eyes of someone we love. The taste of apple cider or popcorn or, better yet, the kisses of a lover. Hearing, smell, touch, sight, taste . . . such a scene is sensual because it offers a banquet for each of the five senses.

The best memories in life are like that, aren't they? Those memories we look back on and can recall vividly and with passion are usually moments in which three or four or even all five of our senses were gainfully employed.

This is sensuality at its best.

I think sensuality has gotten a bad rap. People tend to link sensuality, always and only, with sexuality. Yet sexuality is only one small part of sensuality. Sensuality *can* lead to sex, but, quite frankly, some of the very best sensual moments don't.

Walking in the rain can be sensual.

Holding and breastfeeding a baby can be sensual.

Listening to music by candlelight can be sensual.

Wearing your favorite sweats—the ones that are baggy and fleecy and worn in just the right spots (despite looking like something the cat dragged in)—can be sensual.

Having afternoon tea with your favorite women friends in an antique shop where lilting music and the scent of potpourri fill the air, well, that's a feast for the senses any day.

Sense-less Living

In our age of convenience, we can go long periods of time without really exercising our senses at all. Our homes, businesses, and cars are climate-controlled to reduce our exposure to the elements. While past generations worked with their hands, most of us today work with our brains. I don't even have to leave my house for days, even weeks, at a time; I can work by modem, shop by phone, and earn a college degree on closed-circuit TV.

As some days draw to a close, and I realize that I've spent all day at my desk and all evening half-asleep in front of the TV, it dawns on me that I've hardly moved a muscle or experienced any interesting or unusual stimuli to any of my five senses. My guess is that you've had similar days as well.

As a nation, I believe that our senses are atrophying from disuse.

A number of years ago I experienced a pretty unnerving bout with depression. The causes of it are not important here; perhaps that is a story for another book another day. But what I would like to say here is that the most devastating symptom of my experience was simply my complete inability to feel. My five external senses, as

Unless life touches us in tangible ways, we're missing out on something grand.

well as internal gauges like happiness, sadness, anger, and desire, had simply clicked into the off position. I felt nothing. I wanted to feel nothing. I had withdrawn to some internal place where I could not touch or be touched, hear or be heard, see or be seen.

There were a number of milestones during my recovery, but one that stands out in my mind is the night I stepped onto our back porch to feed Misty Penny, our golden retriever, and I had this urge to . . . well, run. Not run away or escape—although I'd fought that urge before—but just *run*.

Our house sits on nearly an acre, and the backyard is bordered by evergreens that loom tall and black when the sun goes down and the stars come out to play. Chased by Misty Penny, I ran toward the trees at the back of the lot. Overhead, the stars glimmered like diamonds against black velvet, and the cold January night air stung my face and arms and lungs. The moon, hung like a silver earring in the sky, illuminated my crazy path as I spun and ran circles in the grass. I watched my breath hang misty and white before me. I smelled promise in the air. The only sounds I heard were the panting of my dog and the thick silence of the night.

That was the first time I knew—I really knew—that I was going to be okay. Looking back, my wild midnight run was marked by an awakening of my five senses, but it was also marked by the first stirrings of hope and joy that I had experienced in a very, very long time.

Life is meant to be experienced: felt, smelled, seen, touched, tasted. Unless life touches us in these real and tangible ways, we're missing out on something grand. I know, because I've been there, and it's a place to which I have no desire to return.

You may not have ever experienced clinical depression. Then again, perhaps you have. Either way, I believe the vast majority of us are living with depressed senses. Fortunately, recovery from this ailment is not as long or tedious as recovery from emotional depression. With a little effort, we can reawaken our physical senses and begin to experience life in vibrant new ways. This sensual reawakening is not exclusively sexual, although as we begin to arouse our senses in nonsexual ways we will certainly find ourselves more alert and alive in sexual situations as well.

How Our Physical Senses Influence Our Emotional Moods

The emotional landscape of a woman is complex terrain. There is no simple map that can in one quick sweep represent the intricacies of mind, spirit, and body that govern the fluctuations in our moods and emotions.

At the risk of oversimplifying a decidedly nonsimple subject, let me make an observation: Our five physical senses provide one of the keys that unlock and influence our emotions.

You know this is true. Perhaps it is the refrain of an old song that can always take you back to the days you and your husband cut classes in order to "make out" in the front seat of his Ford Pinto. Maybe it's the sensation of contentment evoked each Thanksgiving when you smell the aroma of pumpkin pie baking to perfection in your oven. We all have sensory triggers that are linked, through some experience we have had in the past, to positive emotions and negative ones as well.

Not being particularly prone to masochism, I'd like to suggest that we focus on the positive emotions. What are some of the sensory experiences that evoke our most pleasurable emotions? Read the examples I've provided, and then go ahead and ponder the question for yourself. You may want to write down your thoughts on a piece of paper.

"What makes me feel maternal?"

How about the *smell* of talcum and lotion on a baby • the *feel* of a toddler's chubby hand in mine • the *smell* of breast milk • the *tug* of a newborn's mouth at my nipple and the *feel* of her warm, sleepy body relaxing in the crook of my arms • how about the *smell* and *taste* of oatmeal cookies I've just pulled, hot, from the oven • then there's the *smell* of yeast and the *feel* of my hands immersed in baking flour • and the *sound* I hear when my daughter cuts loose and laughs hysterically with the wild, teary-eyed abandon that comes so easily to children.

Now it's your turn. What sensory triggers evoke motherly feelings in you?

"What makes me feel nurtured?"

I think about the *warmth* derived from cupping my hands around a mug of hot herbal tea • the *touch* of the breath of steam against my face and the *aroma,* faintly sweet and nutty, of the brew • how about the *feel* of my favorite faded jeans coupled with my thickest pair of socks • or the *taste* and *texture* of a Hershey's Kiss dissolving in my mouth.

What about you? What makes you feel nurtured?

"What makes me feel safe?"

I like the *sound* of the rain on the roof of my house • the crackling *sounds* and pungent *smell* of a fire in the hearth • the rhythmic *sound* of my husband breathing in sleep beside me at night • how about the pillowy *touch* of a goose down comforter • or the *sight* of smoke curling from a chimney or the way, at dusk, the lights in a house beckon yellow and warm.

What senses evoke a sense of safety for you?

"What makes me feel alive?"

The bite of cold air on my *skin* • the *smell* of fall • the *sight* of November leaves turning yellow and red and gold • the snappy *taste* of orange marmalade • the *sounds* of a high school marching band practicing at dusk • the *touch* of snowflakes on my cheek • the *sight* of my daughter rollerblading in the driveway.

Now it's your turn. What makes you feel alive?

"What makes me feel feminine?"

The *fragrance* of Red Door cologne • the *taste* of white chocolate • the *brush* against my body of silk panties or a new bra with lots of lace • the *melody* of music played on a hammered dulcimer • the *smell* of potpourri or a scented candle, preferably vanilla or peach • the *sound* of a small group of my favorite women friends laughing • the *feel* of a long-stemmed glass between my thumb and fingers.

What about you? What sensory delights enhance your feelings of femininity?

Orchestrating Ensembles of Sensations

Reread my lists and yours as well. What a feast for the senses! Of course, some of these experiences—like rain on the roof or the coming of fall—can't be manipulated into being. They happen on their own timetable and it is up to you and to me to adjust our busy schedules to enjoy these moments when they come. Other experiences are created by us and can be arranged as frequently as we desire.

We know that our bodies work better if we submit them to vigorous exercise three times a week for a minimum of twenty minutes. That kind of schedule isn't realistic when it comes to exercising our senses, but the principle certainly can apply. What would happen if we made a conscious effort to exercise our senses—perhaps just minutes at a time—three or four times a day? Better yet, how much could our lives be enhanced if we made an effort to *combine* sensual moments?

For example, the next time it rains, turn off the TV or take a break from balancing your checkbook. While you listen to the rain dancing on the roof, drink herbal tea, and enjoy something chocolatey. Suddenly you don't have an isolated melody—you have created a harmonic ensemble of sensations designed to achieve the same goal: to help you feel safe and nurtured.

Even better, find a way to combine experiences that evoke contrasting moods. Before you surround yourself with sensations of safety and comfort, expose yourself to sensations that will make you feel alive: Leave your umbrella at home, pull on a bright yellow raincoat, and take a brisk walk in the rain. Then when you come home to tea and chocolate, all of your senses will be heightened by the contrast.

Other examples of contrasting sensations might include going to the gym and working your muscles toward new boundaries, then pampering those muscles in a hot whirlpool.

Spend a Saturday afternoon lounging languidly at a poolside, basking in the sun, half-naked and slippery with sunscreen—then shower and dress to the hilt and take your husband to a ritzy restaurant, and you will heighten

Leave your umbrella at home and take a brisk walk in the rain.

the contrasts in your day. (I'll admit, this isn't the typical weekend for most married couples with children, but it's a great idea for one of your weekends away.)

The church I attended as a kid owned a mountain camp where I spent a number of memorable summer weeks. The camp boasted a spring-fed lake in which the water was always fresh and freezing cold. The lake had actually been a gravel quarry before mountain waters filled it to the brim. There was no beach—deep water began immediately and a diving board helped campers to be embraced by that deep water in a rather prompt and immediate fashion. Of course, campers in the pursuit of comfort—that is, parents—could swim in a heated pool or relax in a Jacuzzi just across an asphalt road from the lake. Naturally, we teenagers attending church camp managed to merge these recreations in a hair-raising fashion. The rage was to spend ten or fifteen minutes in the Jacuzzi until your body felt like it was on the verge of a meltdown and then to race, dripping, across the hot asphalt, clamber up the diving board, and drop like a cannonball into the icy black waters.

The shock was immeasurable. The cold water turned to fire and burned our skin. We bobbed, gasping and sometimes screaming good-naturedly, every nerve ending alive and throbbing for a moment before the numbing cold set in.

And then we'd climb out and do it again.

It's an extreme example of contrasting sensations and, to be honest, sounds like the kind of experience that can be truly enjoyed only prior to puberty. Or during a menopausal hot flash—*maybe*. But that's about it. Nevertheless, I'm sure you get the idea.

Orchestrate contrasts.

Surprise your senses.

Experience life.

So What Does This Have to Do with Sex?

Amazing. Eight pages and nary a word about sex.

Here's why:

I can promise you that

- if you make a conscious effort to exercise and enjoy your five senses on a daily basis

- if you look for ways to orchestrate ensembles of sensation
- if you stretch your physical boundaries beyond comfortable and sedentary living

then you will have laid the groundwork for more sensual sexuality.

You can build on that foundation by finding new ways to stimulate your senses during lovemaking. For example, there are lots of ways to introduce new sounds into your lovemaking; cassette tapes or CDs of instrumental or ethnic music or even nature tapes with sounds of thunderstorms, forest birds, or the surf breaking against the shore may enhance your sensual experience.

What about new textures or new ways to touch? Borrow the feather boa from your daughter's box of dress-up clothes and incorporate it into one of your more sexually sensual moments (I'll let you use your imagination on this one). Wait for your local department store's January white sale and splurge on satin sheets. Buy a bottle of massage oil and introduce a back rub or body massage into your lovemaking. An all-lace bra or silky nightgown will provide new texture as well.

On this topic of exploring touch and texture with your spouse, author Jennifer Louden suggests shampooing each other's hair: "Enjoy the feel of the hair between your fingers, the feel of the fingers in your hair, the tactile rubbing, the smell of the shampoo. Pause frequently and breathe deeply to give both of you time to enjoy all the sensations" *(The Woman's Comfort Book)*. She goes on to add:

> Separately, select some objects with different textures: a peeled orange, silk shirt, feathers, ice cubes, eggs. Decide who will go first. Blindfold your partner and take turns putting items into hands or under feet, against elbows or behind knees. You can get as involved (and

messy) as you wish. Have your partner guess what he or she is feeling. You can write down answers and compare notes later. If you wish, make it into a game, where the person with the most correct guesses wins. (The prize is up to you.)"

What about sight? Try experimenting with different levels of lighting. A friend of mine admitted that one night she and her husband made love by flashlight. Or restrict sight completely and all the other senses will be intensified.

New smells can be easily introduced with perfumes or colognes or scented candles. Finding new tastes during lovemaking requires a bit of imagination. In the first years

It's a miracle the Dr. Pepper didn't spill all over the bed. The Pringles, unfortunately, did.

of my marriage I bought tutti-fruiti flavored massage oil; it wasn't a big hit for us, but you might have a different experience. Last week I saw advertised in a catalog chocolate body paint—another idea for the adventurous. Certain foods are considered sensual: strawberries, grapes, chocolate. Bring some into bed (notice I didn't suggest crackers) and feed each other.

By the way, as you introduce new sensations to yourself and to your husband, you don't have to take yourself too seriously. Have fun. Laugh a little. A few months ago I was feeling stressed-out over a project when my husband appeared at the bedroom door carrying a tray. It contained a rather unusual combination of "sensual" foods along with some of our daily favorites. That's how

I ended up concluding a rather hectic day by sitting in bed drinking Dr. Pepper and eating grapes and Pringles. Actually, I wasn't allowed to eat the grapes myself; Larry insisted on feeding them to me. Oh yes, he also had found a small bamboo fan from China that he waved in my face as he popped grapes into my mouth. We were laughing so hard it's a miracle the Dr. Pepper didn't spill all over the bed. The Pringles, unfortunately, did.

Take Care of Your Body

I believe one of the best ways to live sensuously—in the bedroom and beyond—is to take care of your body. Nutrition and exercise greatly affect our ability to experience the many sensations that life has to offer. Earlier I mentioned experiencing emotional depression. One of the many keys to the regaining of my well-being was a period of roughly three months during which I completely eliminated added sugars and fat from my diet. Suddenly I had greater energy. I could think more clearly. My five physical senses were heightened. My emotional demeanor improved as well.

Despite our perception of sugar as a giver of energy, following a brief spurt of energy, sugar actually depresses our physical systems and our emotions as well. It is, in fact, classified by some experts as a drug. Sugar not only alters our moods; we can become physically addicted to it. If we want to experience life to its fullest, it won't help to live our lives drugged by the altering effects of too much sugar in our systems.

For that matter, any "medicating" substance that we ingest to numb the harsh edges of life will result in less sensuous living. Alcohol, drugs, and food are among the culprits that can leave us too anesthetized to seek out the sensations that life has to offer.

On the other hand, exercise can make us more sensual beings by readying our bodies—physiologically and psychologically—for the sensations available to each of us. In addition to increasing the flow of blood and oxygen to nerves and muscles, exercise:

- improves mental attitude
- increases self-confidence
- speeds up metabolism
- builds strength and stamina
- encourages better nighttime sleep
- increases energy levels
- and enhances overall physical and mental awareness

Do you want to live more sensuously? Your body is the avenue by which you are able to experience the sensations of life around you. Your body is also the temple of the Holy Spirit. With a little self-care, you can stay alert and tuned and ready for all that God wants you to experience and to accomplish in your years on earth.

Fantasize about Your Spouse

I'll admit that I've already taken some flak on this chapter. One friend suggested that this chapter can't be *biblical*—after all, aren't there verses against this sort of thing?

Another friend, married for fifteen years, suggested that this chapter might be biblical but that it's certainly not very practical. She said that the whole point of fantasy is to go somewhere—do something—in your mind that is unavailable to you in real life. She said that husbands were just too . . . available . . . to be viable objects of fantasy. She said no one would actually *fantasize* about a *husband.*

At the risk of offending my very spiritual friends and my pragmatic friends as well, I beg to differ. I believe that fantasizing about the man whose underwear you fold is both biblical and possible. We can fantasize about our spouses, we can do it with biblical integrity, and we can do it in a way that will enhance our marriages.

Can Fantasy Be Biblical?

There is no question that the Bible speaks out strongly regarding lustful thoughts and vain imaginations. Indeed, many fantasies fit all too neatly into these two categories. It doesn't take a lot of analysis, for example, to figure out that romantic or sexual daydreams about someone other than your spouse are displeasing to God. I mean, this is a no-brainer. Jesus simply couldn't have said it any plainer: "You have heard that it was said, 'Do not commit adultery.' But I tell you that anyone who looks at a woman lustfully has already committed adultery with her in his heart" (Matthew 5:27–28 NIV).

Despite the gender-specific wording, this verse applies to you and to me as well. It's a strict standard, I agree, especially living in a world where titillating images confront us at every turn. And yet God is not in the business of creating tough standards on a whim. His righteous standards glorify him and protect you and me as well. For starters, God knows that impure thoughts can hinder our prayers (Psalm 66:18 NIV). They can render us "unclean" and lead to destructive behaviors including sexual immorality, theft, murder, and adultery (Mark 7:20–21 NIV). Finally, a heart that devises "wicked imaginings" is one of seven things that are hated by God (Proverbs 6:18 NIV).

For these reasons and more, we are instructed to guard our thoughts. One of my favorite passages establishes a pretty clear standard when it comes to the caliber of thoughts that should be admitted past the gatekeeper of our hearts and minds: "Finally, brothers, whatever is true, whatever is noble, whatever is right, whatever is pure, whatever is lovely, whatever is admirable—if anything is excellent or praiseworthy—think about such things" (Philippians 4:8 NIV).

May It Please the Court . . .

Given all this, if I were defending my initial proposal in a court of law, I would at this moment rise to address the judge and jurors and say something along these lines: "May it please the court, I would like to submit that while there is a *category* of fantasy that is displeasing to God—no, actually *hated* by God—*not all fantasy can be viewed in this light.* There are, indeed, fantasies in which we can engage that are pleasing to God, that are healthy and biblical, and that can actually draw us closer to becoming the godly women that God had in mind when he crafted us with such tender care!"

Fantasy. Webster defines it as unrestrained imagination. In our society, we frequently think of fantasy as referring to *sexual* fantasy—and yet the word is pregnant with such greater meaning!

Think of it—unrestrained imagination. What a wonderful concept. I would wager that, given this definition, God engaged in his share of fantasy in order to accomplish the creationary feats that marked the first week on earth. First he imagined, and then he created, the heavens and the earth and darkness and light, land and sea and stars and moon, fish and birds and creeping things. And then he imagined, and he created, a man and then a woman, and through them the miracle of love and the miracle of new life. What an epic extravaganza of fantasy marked the birth of the world and of humankind!

This, then, was our beginning—and our legacy. Do you realize that our imaginations are an inheritance from our heavenly Father? The ability to imagine, to ponder, to meditate, to think creatively, to harness the power of our very thoughts are gifts not to be taken lightly.

And yet don't we do just that? How often have we prefaced or concluded a statement with the disclaimer, "It was just a thought . . ."?

Just a thought!

If only we knew.

The truth is that the power of our thoughts is . . . well, it's mind boggling. For example, did you know that scientists have proven that the brain cannot tell the difference between something that is actually experienced and something that is imagined vividly and in great detail? Athletes know that when practice on the field isn't possible, they can hone their skills by visualizing themselves successfully performing the feat they want to perfect. In other words, bowling a strike, nailing a perfect landing on a complicated vault, lobbing the power pass that lands

> *The brain cannot tell the difference between something experienced and something imagined vividly.*

the winning touchdown, each of these skills can be refined in the mind. This in turn becomes the very blueprint that the brain will later use to direct the performance of the body.

The proverb "As a man thinketh in his heart, so is he" is aptly true. Our thoughts shape our attitudes and, eventually, our very actions. This is not contrary to Scripture but is directly in line with biblical thought. In fact, I believe it was the intimate knowledge of this very working of the human mind that prompted Jesus' comparison of *thinking* about committing adultery with the actual *act* of infidelity. As the craftsman of the human mind, Jesus knew that thinking and acting aren't so very different after all.

Imagination and Matrimony: The Bad News

Given the incredible power of our thoughts, there are lots of ways we can let our imagination tear down our marriages. Fantasizing about sexual or romantic situations outside of our marriages is just one of the destructive options we have!

Another is something I call fantasizing about the faults of our spouses. That's right! Dwelling incessantly on the faults and foibles of men has provided a lot of fodder for female comedians. What makes us laugh so hard at their observations is that many of us have spent hours pondering the same questions and voicing the same criticisms! I'll admit that there are times we all deserve and can benefit from some constructive criticism, but wives—and husbands!—need to be careful not to develop a destructive pattern of nursing negative thoughts about their spouses and their marriages.

There is a third way our imaginations can impair our marriages. Let's say I'm in the mood for a romantic fantasy. I spend an hour daydreaming about a romantic encounter with a man who woos me with flowers and delights in fulfilling my every unspoken sexual need. Because I know better than to fantasize about someone other than my husband, I plaster his face on my dreams. I tell myself my fantasy is about my husband, but in reality, the man in my mind bears no resemblance to the man who sleeps in my bed each night, who happens to think that flowers are a waste of money, and who has never been particularly good at reading my mind and discerning those "unspoken sexual needs." This kind of fantasy can lead to disappointment and disillusionment when the real man in my life continues to fall short of his counterpart who lives in my mind.

Even though this chapter is entitled "Fantasize about Your Spouse," doing so shouldn't mean nurturing wildly unrealistic images that can raise our expectations far beyond the ability of any ordinary man to fulfill!

So what *does* it mean? How *can* we use our imaginations in ways that will refine and enhance our marriages?

Imagination and Matrimony: The Good News at Last!

In preparing for this chapter, I took a break from my research and writing and called my parents in California. They are friends as well as parents, and talking with them always provides a refreshing change of pace. Recently my conversation with my mom provided something even more—inspiration for this particular chapter.

You see, it was their thirty-sixth wedding anniversary. That's more than three-and-a-half decades of living and loving and learning the ropes of how to make a marriage work over the long haul. Not a small accomplishment in an age where the average Maytag washing machine lasts longer than the average marriage!

In light of the milestone that she and my dad crossed, I asked my mom for a little advice. I asked her how a woman might go about using her imagination in ways that would enhance, sexually and otherwise, her relationship with her husband.

In answering my question, my mom based her words on nearly four decades of hard-won wisdom, and from her words I derived the following seven principles. You'll notice that I've arranged them according to days of the week, although there is certainly no need to attempt to fit all seven of these approaches into a single week. Each is, in fact, potent in its own right; indeed, I believe that any one of the following principles, applied with passion to your thought life, will make a difference in your marriage. Apply all seven, and you and your man may never be the same again.

Monday: Dwell on Fact, Not Fiction

Let's face it: There's nothing pretty about denial. As powerful as our thoughts and words may be, telling yourself over and over again that you are married to Prince Charming when your man is in fact a frog will not—I repeat, will not—transform him from the amphibian that he is. Rather than dwell on thoughts or scenarios that are far-flung from your personal reality, select five thoughts that are a positive yet truthful representation of your life and make a conscious effort to meditate on these thoughts throughout the day.

A friend of mine, for example, recalls a time when she fell headlong out of love with her husband. After several years of a troubled marriage, she awoke one morning to find she had lost any loving feelings for him. In the beginning, her thoughts were filled with dark and bitter interpretations of her marriage. "I married the wrong man," she told herself. "I will never find happiness." "I am trapped forever!"

When she realized that these thoughts were merely exacerbating an already dim situation, she shifted gears. Unfortunately, she tried to bulldoze over her reality by thinking positive thoughts that were, in fact, little more than exercises in denial: "We're a happy couple," "I have a great marriage," and "I am madly in love with my husband," were a few of the phrases she repeated to herself daily.

These phrases—all lies—rang hollow, and eventually this woman began to look for more truthful observations that might instill her with some solid hope. Soon her

Telling yourself you're married to Prince Charming when your man is a frog will not transform him from the amphibian he is.

thought list began to look like this: "Even though the past three years have been hard, we had eight good years together and I know, with some work, we can recapture what we once had." "Our problems may take some work—counseling, literature, prayer, better communication—but they are not insurmountable." "God is able and willing to restore harmony and love back into my marriage." "I am willing to do all that is within my power to improve my marriage." "My marriage is worth fighting for." And so on. Looking back, she says today that her optimistic and realistic new thought life marked the beginning of a phase of growth and healing in her relationship that helped restore her crumbling marriage.

Select several statements that are accurate yet positive ways of looking at your spouse, your marriage, your sex life, even your image of your body. Write them on a card and meditate frequently on these statements throughout the day.

Tuesday: Consider the Positive Qualities of the Man You Married

Emotionally and sexually, it's hard to be intimate with someone whose faults consume your thoughts daily. Keeping in mind the principle from Monday—dwell on fact, not fiction—find time throughout the day to recognize positive traits of the man you married. Ask yourself the following questions: "What were some of the traits that caused me to fall in love with this person in the beginning?" "What do other people find attractive or positive about my husband?" "What are some of the ways God has gifted the man I married?" Find a moment tonight to compliment your husband on one of these traits.

Wednesday: Ponder Improvements in Increments

For two days we've tried to generate positive thoughts that accurately represent our marriages, our husbands, even ourselves, as they currently exist. This is not to say, however, that there isn't a time and place to think about the future and the way we would *like* things to be in our relationships with our husbands!

The key is to ponder improvement in increments. If your husband is the silent type who thinks a grunt qualifies as a response and three grunts a dissertation make, don't spend mental energy fantasizing about a dinner date in which he spends two hours bearing his soul over prime rib and a Caesar salad. If the gap between reality and fantasy is too great, you have accomplished little other than setting yourself up for disappointment.

Instead, spend fifteen minutes today picturing a scenario that is an incremental improvement over your reality. Perhaps, in your mind's eye, your husband answers one of your questions with four words and six seconds of eye contact to boot! But don't just put your husband in the fantasy; picture yourself as well. What kind of question might you ask that would encourage such a response? If you touched his arm or face gently as you spoke, would it help you get his attention? What place or timing would be most conducive? Is there a time of day when your husband is at his most relaxed and therefore more likely to open up verbally?

Act out several scenarios in your mind, each time placing yourself in the picture. In your imagination, allow yourself to say or do some small thing that would encourage the kind of response you are imagining in your husband. In time, look for an opportunity to treat your husband in real life the way you have been treating him in your fantasies.

Thursday: Meditate on Role Models

My mom told me that when she married, she had a wonderful picture in her mind of what she wanted her marriage to be like. This image had been fostered throughout her years in her parents' home as she observed the intimate and godly marriage of her mother and father.

Not everyone, she admitted, is so privileged. Many men and women enter marriage without ever having seen a positive role model of marriage as it was intended by God. My mom then told me the story of a couple, college friends of my parents, who struggled fiercely in the first few years of their marriage. Neither husband nor wife seemed to have a strong mental picture of what their roles in marriage were supposed to look like, and so they peered around and together selected a more mature couple after whom they might pattern their relationship. They selected my mom's parents as their adopted role models and for years worked hard to visualize themselves treating each other and raising their family the way they saw Demos and Rose go about it all.

The approach did nothing less than revolutionize their marriage. They went on to raise kids, build companies, start ministries. Today they remain happily married, they are prosperous and influential in their community, and it's their turn to provide for their kids, grandkids, and anyone else who cares to observe, a shining example of all that God intends the Christian marriage to be.

Friday: Visualize Better Patterns for Yourself

Forget about your husband. Today, spend some time picturing yourself engaged in thoughts, words, actions, and attitudes that you know would make a positive difference in your marriage.

Does your husband complain that you never initiate sexual intimacy? Picture several scenarios in which you make the first pass.

Do you usually greet your husband at the door by handing him a sticky toddler and growling, "It's your turn!" Take some time and fantasize about some alternatives that might create a smoother transition into intimate evenings together.

Do you tend to relate passively to your husband, storing small hurts and swallowing your anger until any room in which you are together drops ten degrees in temperature? Visualize yourself making small changes in your communication so that you are more honest about your feelings, airing and dispelling small hurts and wounds before they have a chance to create an icy barrier between you and your husband.

Saturday: Reminisce about the Past

My mother recalls a time in her marriage when outside pressures were putting a strain on her relationship with my father. About this time, while cleaning out a drawer, she inadvertently uncovered a cache of pictures taken during the early years of their marriage. One of the pictures in particular tugged on her heartstrings and filled her with remembered joy.

The picture may not seem like much to most. It's a small black and white, poorly composed, faintly out of focus, and faded with age. In it, my dad is sitting on a

Find photos that will kindle warm memories and let them cast their golden glow on your attitudes today.

couch in my grandmother's home. The sleeves on his white dress shirt are rolled up, his tie is crooked, and his eyeglasses are filled with glare where the camera caught him by surprise. In his arms relaxes one of my sisters, a chubby toddler wearing saddle oxfords and sucking her fingers.

What's special about the photo is the period of time it represents—a span of time, my mother recalls, when babies were little and love was good and life was filled with promise. Several decades later, finding that photo in a forgotten box, my mother was reminded of how much in love she and my dad had been and have been throughout their marriage. For her that day, in the face of external pressures and challenges, the depth of her love for my father was rekindled and renewed.

Today my mom keeps the photo on her desk at home, next to two other pictures: one taken of my mother when she was a little girl, perhaps eight years old, and the other taken of my mother's father shortly before he died in 1993. She calls this trio of memories her "comfort pictures." Each one, after all, has the power to take her back to secure and happy days.

Find photos that kindle warm memories for you. Perhaps the photos will be of you, you and your husband, or your husband alone. In any case, put them where you can see them often, and let yesterday's memories cast their golden glow on your attitudes today.

Sunday: Remember Your Husband in Prayer

Last but not least, pray for your husband. Many times during prayer God will drop images into our minds that will guide us in praying for things that he desires for us. In this way, our prayers have the power to reflect back to us things that are being completed in the spiritual realm even though they have yet to be evidenced in the physical realm. After all, our prayers are fueled by faith, which is nothing less than the substance of things hoped for and the evidence of things not seen (see Hebrews 11:1).

Select verses characterizing godly traits you would like to see the Holy Spirit continue to cultivate in your husband. Incorporate these verses into your quiet times with the Lord, "praying" these Scriptures over your husband as he goes about his daily schedule. You may even want to insert his name into the verse as you pray. An example might be taken from Proverbs 19:20. Incorporated into your prayers, the verse might appear like this: "Lord, help my husband to listen to advice and to accept instruction, so that, in the end, he will have wisdom."

All in all, submit your imagination to the Lord. Ask him to guide you in using the power of your thoughts to build up your husband and your marriage.

Give Yourself Permission to Say No to Sex

Recently I received a phone call from a friend as she was getting ready to head out the door to work. She said that her son had an orthodontist appointment at 8:30 and asked if I could possibly pick him up after the appointment was over and take him to school. I agreed and prepared to meet David at the doctor's office shortly after nine.

I enjoy David. At thirteen he is witty and verbal and often observes life a little left of center. I can usually count on him for lively verbal banter, and that particular morning was no exception. As he tossed his backpack onto the floorboard and climbed into the car, I asked what I thought was a pretty innocuous question: "So. You ready for school?"

David gazed out the window in thought. I should have known I was in store for more than the typical adolescent single-syllable grunt.

"Ready?" he repeated. "Well sure, I've got my books and stuff, if that's what you mean. But *ready?* I mean, it's not like anyone gives me a choice about these things. No one comes into my room in the morning and says, 'Hey, David, do you want to go to school or do you want to sleep in and maybe catch a movie later?'" He took a breath but hurried on, on a roll now. "You know, I don't think it counts if you don't have a choice. I mean, if someone *asked* once in a while—not every day, of course, but just once in a while—it might be different. But noooo. It doesn't matter if I'm ready. I have to go. I have to go to school every day." He flung his hands in the air in resignation as he announced, "So . . . here I am."

Indeed, we were pulling into the parking lot of his school at that very moment. David grabbed his stuff and tumbled out the car door in one smooth move. "Thanks for the ride, Mrs. Linamen!" he shouted over his shoulder just before the car door slammed. Then he galloped toward the school door, toward friends and angst and adventure, just another thirteen-year-old with gangly feet and wire mouth and unruly hair . . . and an uncommon knack of seeing the world as it is.

He's right, you know. There's a vast difference between logistical and emotional readiness. Logistical readiness is a little like being drafted into the service; you're there because you have to be.

Emotional readiness, on the other hand, requires something more.

Does Yes Count If I Can't Say No?

Do you know women who are so servant-hearted that they can't seem to say no to any request from family, friends, or organizations? Just like David feels "drafted" into attending junior high, these women have been drafted into service and somehow don't feel they have the right to say no, even when they are teetering on the edge of exhaustion.

I can see you nodding. You might be thinking of someone from your church, your best friend, a room parent at your child's school . . . or maybe the woman who stares back at you from the bathroom mirror each morning.

One of my best friends falls into this category. Baking cookies, teaching Sunday school, administrating Vacation Bible School, organizing a women's luncheon, making meals for a sick friend, coordinating school parties,

Where do we get the idea that it's not okay to say no to sex—ever?

carpooling kids on field trips, helping a friend organize her pantry—I think the only thing she hasn't agreed to do might be patching a leaky roof, but the rainy season's not over yet, so it could still happen.

My friend volunteers for many of these services, and yet even when her schedule is full and she has by anyone's standard gone above and beyond the call of duty, my friend doesn't feel the freedom to say no. The next time she gets a call from church or school or work or a distraught friend, Cherie still says yes. Only this time there's a note of exhaustion in her voice. The next time the phone rings, she says yes again and the caller, without a video phone, never sees the glint of panic in her eyes. I am waiting for the day when the phone rings and Cherie says yes—this time through a speaker phone because her arms are in a straightjacket.

Her husband recently taped a piece of paper to the wall next to the phone. It contains a list entitled "Ten Ways to Say No." And you know what? It's working. The good news is that as Cherie gives herself permission to say no to incoming requests, she is finding that she has more time, energy, and heart to give to the projects she does agree to fit into her busy schedule.

Bedroom Etiquette

What about in our bedrooms? Do any of us feel at times like we have been drafted without our consent into one sexual assignment or another that leaves us feeling empty or trapped? It would be nice to think that with the right transition, any woman could welcome sex at any moment. But life isn't that simple, is it? So what do we do when we *really* don't want to do it? Is it okay to say no? Is it right? It is biblical?

According to my friend Beth, bedroom etiquette at her house goes something like this:

Most of the time when her husband wants to make love, Beth transitions easily into a frame of mind that allows her to enjoy and welcome the encounter.

Then there are times when Beth knows that she is too tired or distracted to enjoy sex, but she makes a willing choice to overlook her lack of desire and to meet the needs of the man she loves.

Finally, there are nights when Beth REALLY isn't in the mood. She feels like saying to her husband simply, "Not now, PLEASE. I'll be ready in an hour or in the morning or tomorrow evening, but right now is really not a good time for me." But instead of saying this, Beth performs. She tells herself it's not okay to refuse her husband in this most sensitive arena. She tells herself he'll be mad or embarrassed or hurt. She tells herself she's not supposed to ever say no. And she resents feeling trapped, and she resents having to pretend.

We *Do* Have a Choice!

Where do we get the idea that it's not okay to say no to sex—ever?

Wait. I think I know. I know because I've heard it quoted by women and by men as well. Check out 1 Corinthians 7:4: "The wife's body does not belong to her alone but also to her husband" (NIV).

Of course, the rest of the verse goes on to say that the husband's body belongs to his wife as well, so that we get a picture of *both* spouses enjoying *equal* privileges in the bedroom. Plus, notice the word "also" in this verse; our bodies belong to our husbands, but they still belong to us as well.

Still, for centuries people have misinterpreted this verse to somehow "prove" that there is some sort of sexual hierarchy in marriage, and that it is the duty of a good wife to make love to her husband at the drop of a hat or dress or pants or whatever.

And yet nowhere else in the Bible is the right to say no stripped so dutifully from a man or woman. In myriad examples and circumstances throughout the pages of Scripture, men and women enjoy options and choices in nearly every arena of their lives.

Church elders, for example, are encouraged to say no to responsibilities at church if their wives and children need them to spend more time at home.

In the fifth chapter of Acts, Ananias and his wife, Sapphira, were given the option of saying no to donating money to the church. What they weren't allowed to do was to donate *part* of the money and then lie, claiming they had given *all*. For this, they paid a "stiff" penalty, dropping dead at the door of the church!

Even Adam and Eve were given the right to say no not just to each other, but to a holy God! How easily our omniscient and omnipotent God could have created Adam and Eve without the freedom to sin. And yet the first man and woman were given the right to say to an omnipotent Creator, "I'm not in the mood to obey you right now." In light of this great freedom, saying to a spouse, "I'm not in the mood to fool around at the moment. . . . Can I take a rain check?" seems like a very small thing indeed!

Free will. Choices. Options. It's a theme that is interwoven time and time again throughout the pages of Scripture. In fact, the greatest example of all is the fact that you and I have the right to say no to the gentle wooing of the Holy Spirit in our lives. God didn't create us as robots, programmed to love and obey and respond to his every whim. This is because he knew that if you and I are not allowed to say no, our *yes* becomes meaningless, academic, moot.

One of the most poignant images in Scripture is that of God the Son, Jesus, all-knowing and all-powerful, standing at the door of our very hearts and knocking gently, asking our permission to enter. No demands. No force. No coercion. Just a question in the form of knuckles tap, tap, tapping on a wooden frame. The answer is up to us. Yes? Or no? We have a choice.

I believe this same imagery can be applied to the intimate relationship between husband and wife. After all, husbands are directed in Scripture to love their wives as Christ loved the church and gave himself up for her.

The letter of the law says that it's okay to be hypocritical in your feelings as long as your performance measures up. The spirit of the law looks at the willingness of your heart. There is nothing spiritual about being pressed into unwilling service. God doesn't want that from us. And neither do our husbands. If the word *no* does not exist in your vocabulary, then *yes* becomes little more than a technicality, and a request no longer is a request, but a demand.

If We Can Say No . . . *How* Should We Say No?

Nobody likes to be turned down. But, believe it or not, there are ways to diffuse the situation and to make your refusal palatable. If you make an executive decision to say no to your husband's bedroom overtures, here are a few suggestions:

DON'T say no to get even or to exert power over your husband. This is a dangerous and destructive approach that will reap discord in your relationship over the long haul. If you are experiencing deep-rooted or long-term anger toward your husband, try to separate these emotions from your sex life. But don't stop there. Find a way to get to the root of the problem and to diffuse your anger, perhaps through prayer, lay counseling or professional therapy, workshops, or support groups.

DON'T rely on nonverbal messages to say no. These can be so easily misinterpreted! Dawdling in the bathroom and coming to bed late, turning your back to your husband, hugging the edge of the bed, pretending to be asleep . . . what are you really saying by these gestures? You might be feeling "nonamorous" for no other reason than menstrual cramps or a headache. Your husband, on the other hand, may be reading much, much more than you intended into your gestures, interpreting your actions to mean that you find him undesirable or, even worse, are somehow repulsed by his overtures.

DON'T *say no via vague excuses.* Once again, these leave too much room for misunderstandings. If your husband gets that glint in his eye and you respond by yawning and saying, "Gee, I'm pretty tired. . . . I'm going to turn in early and I'll bet I'm asleep before my head hits the pillow," you may be simply saying you are too tired for sex. He, on the other hand, may well interpret your message to mean a more personal rejection than you ever intended.

DO *be direct, affirming your husband and confirming your desire for him.* If you are going to make the choice to say no, try reaching out to your husband both physically and

Saying no is not saying no at all, but saying later.

emotionally. Touch his hand or give him a quick snuggle or hug and say something that will let him know that you love him and find him desirable. You might begin by saying: "I know you're feeling romantic, and I love making love to you, but right now . . ."

DO *give a brief reason that explains your temporary need for space.* Following an affirming statement, give a brief reason for your decline. An example might be ". . . but right now isn't a good time for me because I'm feeling really exhausted from getting up six times last night with the baby" or whatever the reason may be.

DO *suggest an alternative "date" when you will be better prepared to welcome and enjoy lovemaking.* Close by saying something like: "I'd really like to make love to you in the morning after I've had some sleep. Can we make a date?" In other words, saying no is not saying no at all, but saying *later.* Together, negotiate another time as soon as possible and let your husband know that you'll be looking forward to that time. Then—and this is important—follow up with enthusiasm when the appointed time arrives. If your "date" arrives and your husband doesn't initiate, make sure you do! He might be feeling tentative after your previous decline and wondering if you really want him as much as he wants you. Let him know that you do!

What happens when we give ourselves permission to say no (or later) to sex? The benefits include:

Avoiding resentment. There is nothing that will build a wall faster in a relationship than resentment, which can haunt women who feel as though their feelings don't matter and that they are "choiceless" when it comes to having sex with their husbands.

Dispelling martyrdom. How much fun can lovemaking be for the man who feels as though he is embracing a suffering martyr! For your husband's self-esteem as well as your own, don't be an unwilling sexual participant when you would rather be doing something—anything!—else. Like it or not, your feelings will be picked up by your husband. No one—regardless of how amorous he might be feeling—appreciates being a charity case.

Fostering honesty. James, in his epistle to the churches, encourages believers to "let your 'Yes' be yes, and your 'No,' no" (James 5:12 NIV). If your husband knows that you can be honest enough to say no when you really feel like saying no, then he will have more confidence that your yes indeed means yes. There will be no need to second-guess, wondering if you find him desirable or if you are consenting out of obligation.

Sex and Self-Sacrifice

Having said all that, let me say a few words about a little something called self-sacrifice.

It really is okay to say no to sex.

But it's also okay to say to yourself, "My husband is feeling romantic and I'm not . . . so what am I going to do about it? Of course, I could choose to say no, or I could choose to focus on my husband's needs instead of my own and to give him the gift of my love tonight. Mmmm . . . I think I'll choose the latter."

There is a principle here, and it is this: If you give yourself permission to say no, you have also given yourself permission to say yes even when you're not quite in the mood. You have given yourself permission to make an unselfish choice and to consider your husband's needs, on any given night, as more important than your own. You have allowed yourself the privilege of making a small sacrifice for someone you love. The best marriages, in fact, are filled with moments such as these, shining moments of self-sacrifice on the part of both partners!

Perhaps the principles can be best summarized in three scenarios. When it comes to the privilege of sexual intimacy in marriage:

- Say YES when you want to make love.
- Say YES when you don't want to make love but when it will bring you joy to meet the needs of your husband.
- Say LATER when making love at that very moment will leave you feeling trapped or resentful.

Sexual intimacy is a gift. It is a gift that God gives to husbands and wives to enjoy, and it is a gift that husbands and wives give to each other. It is a gift that deserves to be unwrapped and cherished in the best possible settings, settings in which integrity, healthy boundaries, and loving sacrifice go hand in hand.

Help Yourself to Greater Femininity

Cindy Crowe is a former college roommate of mine, one of three friends with whom I shared lodgings, laughter, and chocolate chip cookie dough at Biola University in the late seventies/early eighties. Several years ago she flew from California to Texas for a visit, which turned into an impromptu reunion of sorts since another member of the fearsome foursome, Bonnie Bell, just happens to live with her family a few miles from my home.

Upon Cindy's arrival we promptly set our minds to having a grand ol' time (despite the regrettable absence of the fourth musketeer, Becky Thayer), and being as we were in Texas, somehow the words *boot-scootin'* formed on our lips.

Cindy wanted to go line dancing.

Our husbands declined our invitations, both hailing from the "We-Wouldn't-Dance-If-There-Were-Ants-in-Our-Pants" school of thought. And so we girls went solo. We drank Dr. Pepper, learned the Achy-Breaky-Heart and came home intoxicated with camaraderie, feeling brave and bonded, enthralled with our friendship and with the adventure we had just shared.

It didn't turn me into a cowboy-bar junkie, but it was a fun night to remember. Best yet, the companionship of women friends left me feeling nurtured in some small corner that is decidedly feminine; some quiet place in the soul that even husbands are challenged to try to reach.

It's taken me a long time to acknowledge the existence of such a place in the spirit. After all, for the first years of my marriage I was under the tragic misperception that my husband was the only legitimate source of all good things in my life. I looked to him to fulfill all my needs for friendship, for romance, for direction in decision making, and for emotional support when I was feeling blue. He was, after all, my knight in shining armor. I expected nothing less than for him to be my protector, my lover, my counselor, my friend, and even my court jester from time to time.

As if this weren't enough of a burden for him to carry, I began looking to him for my sense of feminine confidence. His words, his responses to me, his actions toward me became my sole source of how I perceived myself as a woman.

I realize now that my fantasies about marriage—and about the source of my feminine identity—were unrealistic. I was foisting on my poor husband a responsibility so fearsome and impossible that it's a wonder he didn't develop some sort of chronic rash or annoying facial tic.

I'm not alone, however, in my delusions. I know too many women who make the same mistake. Somehow, we get this idea that the men in our lives are supposed to be our all in all—that somehow they are the sources of our happiness, that they have the power to fulfill all our needs. What's more, it's up to them to make us feel pretty, feminine, nurtured, pampered, fulfilled, desirable.

What *are* we *thinking?* Thank heaven our husbands don't put the same demands on us. No, men tend to get their sense of self-esteem and masculine confidence from a variety of sources: their careers, financial accomplishments, athletics, hobbies, competitive razzing with male buddies, and, yes, their wives. I'm glad I'm represented on the list; I'm also glad I do not single-handedly comprise the list. Imagine the pressure I'd live with if I knew I was the sole source of my husband's masculinity! Yet this is the burden we too often heave onto the broad but human shoulders of the men we love.

Beautiful Women Still Get the Blues

Just as some women rely on the men in their lives to "make" them feel feminine, other women harvest their sense of femininity from physical attributes they may or may not possess. One of my friends, for example, admits that she grew up convinced she wasn't very feminine because her bustline was smaller than that of the women her dad ogled on the street and in the pages of *Playboy*. She remembers: "My dad always commented on women with large breasts, and he read pornography. I grew up thinking that's what I was supposed to look like. As a result, my self-esteem was in the pits until I became a Christian. When I met Jesus, however, and discovered that God's ways are different from the ways and thoughts of the world, I found a new source of esteem. I realized my femininity was a gift from God. It was determined by him and not by the size of my Wonderbra."

On the other hand, we've all known strikingly beautiful women—yes, women with enviable bustlines and more—who are equally dogged by anemic self-esteem and puny gender confidence. Why? I've got a couple theories on this one: First, think about the fact that cover girl looks can put a woman more frequently in competition with other women, robbing her of the feminine companionship meant to nurture her softer side.

Second, consider the long-term effects of frequent flirtations from men. Women who attract men like bees to pollen may learn to derive their sense of femininity from the attention they draw. That sounds fine, except for the fact that building our esteem wholly on external sources is pure folly. Women whose sense of femininity depends on their ability to be beautiful and attract men are walking on thin ice. Their beauty, thus used, becomes a fragile crutch; the fragility of that crutch can leave them more vulnerable than other women with, say, a more moderate dose of good looks.

And the Survey Says . . .

There is a third source from which too many of us clone our thoughts about womanhood in general and our personal femininity as well.

That source, of course, is public opinion as it is portrayed in the media. For better or worse, the books/movies/TV shows/magazine articles/celebrity opinions to which we are exposed do much to influence our perception of what it means to be a real woman.

Plant Your Own Garden

Contrary to what I may have implied in the previous paragraphs, there's nothing wrong with being influenced by the opinions and responses of those around us. After all, the positive appraisal in the eyes of a stranger as we pass on the street *does* give our confidence a small boost. Receiving praises and compliments from our husbands should, indeed, massage our esteem. The values modeled by our parents as we were growing up were—hopefully—mostly constructive and do, without a doubt,

It's us that makes us feel feminine. A man can't do it for us.

shape the way we view ourselves, our gender, and our world. Likewise, the values of the society in which we live play a role in our belief systems as well.

The problem arises when we look to these external sources as the sole genesis of our feminine esteem.

Think of the whole scenario in terms of . . . well, vegetables. Imagine yourself living in a time before grocery stores and farmers markets. (I know it's not easy—go back to cave days if you have to.) Luckily, you have a number of friends who like to garden and who keep you supplied with their overabundance of harvest. You've never hefted a hoe in your life, but you nevertheless enjoy a bounty of fresh veggies nearly daily. Of course, you have cause to complain a little now and then when your friends pass the slug-eaten surplus on to you and keep the prize-winning produce for themselves.

And occasionally they get busy with other things in their lives and forget to give you any vegetables at all.

And once in a while you wish you knew how to raise a few beans for yourself so you wouldn't feel so needy or dependent.

But overall, you think it's a pretty good system. Sort of.

I think you get the picture. When it comes to the celebration of our softer side . . . our feelings of femininity . . . our womanly worth . . . there's no need to exist at the mercy of handouts from others. We don't have to starve for affirmation of our worth as women. In the final analysis, you and I are responsible for the health of our feminine identities. It is up to us to cultivate experiences, relationships, and personal perspectives that help us fulfill our potential as the gentler sex. We can put our hands to the plow and begin to "grow" our own feminine esteem, and once we do, we'll never look back.

Mary, Mary, Quite Contrary, How Does Your Garden Grow?

In preparing to write this chapter, I interviewed a number of women about their horticultural secrets. Among the questions I wanted answered were these:

How exactly did they put their femininity into *practice?* In other words, what special rituals or rewards helped them to feel their most feminine? Also, how did they cultivate a lush and healthy *perspective* of themselves as women? And what about *priorities?* How important is it to maintain a strong gender identity? In the face of daily distractions and even crises, how do they keep from losing touch with their feminine characteristics?

Here's what they had to say.

On Practicing Your Femininity

Many of the women I spoke with had favorite rituals that brought out their feminine sides. My sister Renee, for example, spends her days in blue jeans and sweatshirts, chasing and teaching and disciplining and loving her two preschool boys. Since her husband, Harald, is in the military and away from home often, raising two preschoolers alone is a full-time job that leaves little time for luxuries like makeup and earrings. On a recent trip to my house, my sister did manage to paint her nails—and it only took her three days to do it. She painted her right hand on Tuesday and lo and behold, it was Friday before she got to the left. But her favorite ritual—the little luxury that rekindles her feminine side—is a bubble bath after the boys are put to bed.

One of my friends treats herself to manicures. Another friend let her husband choose rugged furniture for their den but reserved the right to decorate their bedroom in ribbons and lace. Still another woman greets each day with a full face of makeup, despite the fact that for much of each day she sees no one but two elementary school children, one toddler, two dogs, and nine guppies. My friend Cherie loves to have tea with friends in an antique tea room in downtown Dallas. She says, "Even if I could talk my husband into going with me, he'd hate it. He's a 'mugger'; teacups drive him crazy. And so when I want to treat myself, I call my girlfriends and we go. It's a woman thing, and we love it. It means having something special to share among ourselves, woman to woman."

What favorite rituals or habits make you feel feminine? What hobbies or little luxuries enrich your bond with the sisterhood of women? No matter what season of life you might find yourself experiencing—newlywed bliss, motherhood midlife, or harvest years—find ways to practice your femininity frequently.

On Perspective

Remember the woman mentioned above? The one whose father was enamored with bustlines? The woman who was confused about her femininity until she became a Christian? Today she speaks frankly about the need for women to get in touch with their Creator before they can truly understand their potential as women.

"God made us, after all," she reflects. "More than anyone else, he knows what it means to be feminine and to be a woman. True femininity requires accepting who we are in Christ and being at peace and comfortable in our role as women. It also means adopting God's perspective on the value of womanhood. Despite what some people think or preach, God didn't make us subservient and second-class, but helpmates and equals. But the key is knowing Christ. Without that relationship with our Creator, we'll never fully grasp the motivation behind his creation. We'll never fully blossom into all that he created us to be."

How can we begin to adopt God's perspective? Reading, studying, and memorizing the Bible gives us God's thoughts in God's own words. Accepting God's gift of salvation through the death and resurrection of Jesus Christ infuses new life into our spirits and lets us enter into a real relationship with God. Prayer brings us into the presence of God and gives us a forum for communication. Godly teaching through church, Bible studies, radio, books, and television helps us expand our knowledge and apply that knowledge in practical ways to our lives. Transparent friendships with other women of faith can leave us encouraged and inspired, providing role models and mentors as we seek to grow into our potential as godly women.

On Making Your Femininity a Priority

In 1982 one woman I know—I'll call her Joyce—underwent a hysterectomy. Nearly fifteen years after the fact, she describes the experience as nothing less than an assault on her femininity. Following the surgery, a combination of dynamics—disruption in hormone production, her body's need to recover from the trauma of surgery, premature menopause, as well as psychological and emotional adjustments—conspired to leave her feeling robbed of her femininity, void of gender, even neutered.

"In the first year after the operation," she remembers, "I experienced a great sense of loss. Things were missing. My uterus was missing from my body, of course. Then, I missed my periods and the regime of feminine hygiene that, for most of my life had, like clockwork, reminded me monthly of my femininity and uniqueness as a woman. My libido also suffered, and I missed the sexual urges and surges that had accompanied my cycle each month. Finally, I felt I was missing some sensation during intercourse. It was puzzling to me. I wondered if nerves had been unintentionally severed during the surgery, or if the lack of sensitivity was because my hormones had been impacted, or psychologically because I knew my uterus was missing. Whatever the reason, my enjoyment diminished."

For months Joyce tried to come to terms with her losses. One year after the surgery she decided she wasn't going to quietly accept what had been handed to her. She'd had enough. She recalls, "Right then I made up my mind to fight for my femininity. I had always loved being sensual and feminine, and I knew I didn't want to settle for something less. I couldn't acquire a new uterus, or regain my menstrual cycles, but there were still things I could do. I wanted my femininity back and I was willing to fight for it."

Joyce began by asking her doctor to put her on hormone therapy, something that hadn't been initiated because her ovaries had been left intact. When he finally consented and she began estrogen and progesterone therapy, she noticed improvements right away.

As another part of her arsenal for reclaiming her femininity, she committed to a daily regimen of exercises. She began with Kegels. Originally designed to help women with bladder control, Kegel exercises boast the desirable side effect of increasing vaginal awareness, sensitivity, and pleasure during lovemaking. You'll find instructions for Kegel exercises, excerpted from the book *Restoring the Pleasure* by Cliff and Joyce Penner (Word, 1993), at the end of this chapter.

She also practiced a second exercise designed to tone and sensitize. To do it, get on your hands and knees. Then, catlike, curve your back into a high arch, tucking

We need to take more advantage of nurturing from other women.

in your tummy and tightening your vagina and buttocks as you go. Hold, then slowly relax these muscles as you lower the arch. Repeat seven to ten more times.

Finally, she made a priority of finding new ways to nurture her feminine side through friendships, hobbies, and personal care. Today, when speaking to other women about reclaiming or developing their sense of femininity, she advises, "Take more advantage of nurturing from other women. There is something about woman-to-woman friendships that can help us stay in touch with our softer sides. Also, certain hobbies can draw out our feminine qualities; wonderful lap dogs, for example, require individual attention that a woman needs to give and receive. Finally, personal care rituals that border on pampering can help a woman feel, think, and act prettier. New clothes, new bedding, new fragrance, a manicure, or pedicure can all rekindle femininity. And even if the money's not there, everyone has a bathtub. With a good soak in a fragrant bath, good brushes and oils, a little classical music and candles, you could pamper yourself and it wouldn't take that much money."

She adds: "There is a certain power of the feminine sex. A lot of times we block it out of ourselves, but the fact is that it's *us* that makes us feel feminine. Every woman has a soft side, and it's up to her to do whatever it takes to stay in touch with that soft side. A man can't do it for you. You have to take responsibility for yourself."

How can we grow our own gardens of gender confidence? Find ways every day to practice your femininity. Strive to adopt God's perspective on the value and significance of your role as a woman. Finally, make your femininity a priority, doing whatever is necessary to discover/reclaim/enhance your softer side.

Your list, by the way, of what it takes to make you feel feminine may look very different from the suggestions given in the preceding paragraphs, and that's okay. (In interviewing women for this chapter, I noticed that no one but me included "boot-scootin' with friends" on their list of Top Ten Feminine Pursuits.) The important thing is to customize your approach. Discern what works for you; then get to work. Begin cultivating the rituals, events, experiences, and relationships that will enable you to celebrate, daily, the profound privilege of being a woman.

Kegel Exercises

Step 1: Identify the sensation of tightening and relaxing the PC (Pubococcygeus) muscle. While sitting on the toilet to urinate, spread your legs apart. Start urination.

Then stop urination for three seconds. Repeat this several times before you are finished emptying your bladder. Some women have difficulty stopping urination. Those women need to work on tightening the PC muscle. Other women need to work on the voluntary relaxing of the PC muscle. If you can do both easily, you only need to tighten and relax the PC muscle twenty-five times per day to keep it in good condition. For those who need to improve the voluntary control of their PC muscle, proceed with the steps below.

Step 2: Do ten to twenty repetitions of this exercise one to four times per day: Gradually tighten the PC muscle tighter and tighter to the count of four. Then hold the muscle as tight as you can while you again count to four. Now gradually relax the muscle, letting go of the tension a little at a time as you count to four.

Step 3: Do ten to twenty repetitions of this exercise one to four times per day: Start to tighten your vagina by thinking of bringing your labia (lips) closer together, like closing an elevator door. Imagine that your vagina is an elevator. You start to tighten at the ground floor. Bring the muscles up from floor to floor, tightening and holding at each floor. Keep your breathing even and relaxed. Do not hold your breath. Go to the fifth floor. Then go down, relaxing the tension of the muscle one floor at a time. When you get to the bottom, bear down as though you are opening the elevator door (the vagina) and letting something out.

Step 4: Do ten to twenty repetitions of this exercise one to four times per day: Rapidly tighten and relax the PC muscle at the opening of the vagina in almost a flickering or fluttering movement.

These exercises will improve vaginal sensation to sexual stimulation, enhance the voluntary tightening and opening of the vagina, and maintain the vagina in better health for more years.

Initiate Sexual Intimacy

There are a lot of reasons to initiate sexual intimacy with your husband other than the fact that it is his birthday and you forgot to buy him a real present. Initiating sex when you are ovulating and trying to get pregnant doesn't count either. Nor does that time you made a pass at your husband right before you told him about the new antique dining-room table you put on layaway.

No, I'm talking about initiating sexual intimacy just for fun.

In talking to various women about this matter, I discovered the following interesting similarities: Every woman I spoke with said her husband would like for her to initiate sex more often than she does. In addition, every woman I spoke with said she, too, would like to initiate sex more often, both for her husband's sake and her own.

So what's the problem? If we'd *like* to be more assertive in the bedroom, what's holding us back?

Among the women I spoke with, reasons for not taking more initiative in the bedroom varied, ranging from not enough interest to not enough confidence to not enough energy.

That's a tough one. Confidence, interest, and energy hardly grow on trees. And yet, I agree, all three are key elements for the woman who wants to successfully seduce her husband.

No Experience, No Job . . . No Job, No Experience

Who can forget those long-ago days and hours spent pursuing that first illusive job? It just didn't seem fair—employers wanted experience, and yet experience couldn't be gained without a job. It was like a merry-go-round from the Twilight Zone. Once you managed to climb aboard, the momentum kept you going; there just never seemed to be a good place to board.

Sex is like that merry-go-round. Without interest, confidence, and energy, it may seem difficult to climb aboard. What many of us tend to forget, however, is that the act of lovemaking has a momentum of its own. Sex doesn't just require interest, confidence, and energy—it *generates* interest, confidence, and energy as well.

I saw a cartoon once that depicted a battle-weary chieftain in full war gear, standing in a tent and gesturing impatiently to his second-in-command. Behind the tent the battle raged, men and horses and swords clashing in cartooned fury. Just outside the tent, in anachronistic detail, stood a salesman in a polyester suit, waiting patiently, his arms cradling the merchandise he was hoping to peddle: nothing other than a machine gun.

As the chieftain berated his second-in-command, the caption read: "You idiot, don't you realize we're losing this battle? I don't have *time* to see a salesperson!"

I loved this cartoon because it was a poignant reminder of how I live a lot of my life! Too often the very thing I

Exercising our libido can strengthen our sex drive. The more we do it, the more we want to do it.

most desperately need and want is the very thing I pass over in haste.

I say I don't have enough energy to go to the gym for the workout that would energize me for days.

I say I'm too lonely to go to the social event that would put me in contact with new friends and acquaintances.

I say I don't have time to read the book on organization that would help me tame my beast of a schedule.

And, unfortunately, like the women interviewed for this chapter, I too say I don't have the confidence, interest, or energy to initiate the sexual encounters that would do nothing less than—you guessed it!—boost my confidence and interest and energy.

The Benefits of Great Sex

This concept that the act of love can bolster your libido, your self-assurance, and your energy and improve your life in general is more than fairy-tale thinking or wishful thinking. There is a growing field of science studying the impact of sex on our physical and emotional wellbeing, and the results are fascinating!

Lovemaking, as it turns out, can boost the production of beneficial hormones, decrease stress, and relieve PMS. And that's just for starters! Let's take a look at a few of the more common reasons women give for not initiating or agreeing to sex—and how lovemaking may actually prove to be the perfect prescription for the very ills that threaten to prevent it!

Problem: "I'm Just Not in the Mood."
Solution: Do It for Your Libido!

According to Dr. Patricia Love, author of *Hot Monogamy* (Dutton, 1994), our interest in sex is determined largely by our hormones. She says that while desire can indeed be influenced by upbringing, gender conditioning, and other psychological and social factors, "only when we examine the role played by sex hormones do we get the complete picture."

And yet the fact that our hormones determine sex drive is really only half the picture. The other half is that lovemaking can help determine the hormonal balance in our bodies. According to an article in *Redbook,* intercourse generates "hormones that tune passion and keep lust alive" ("Sexual Healing," April 1993). Dr. Dudley Chapman, a professor at Ohio University College of Osteopathic Medicine, explains that "sex boosts production of dopamine, the primary hormone of desire."

It's true that there are simply times we're just not in the mood for sex, regardless of whose idea it is. And yet it doesn't hurt to keep in mind that exercising our libido, over time, strengthens our sex drive. It's the old "use it or lose it" concept. Indeed, the more we do it, the more we *want* to do it.

Problem: "But I Don't Feel Sexy." Solution: Do It for Your Confidence!

Bedroom confidence can be linked to a lot of things. One of my friends is an attractive and slender blonde who has an easy grace about her and an easy smile too. Of all things, she says a lack of confidence about her *appearance* is the thing that keeps her from taking more sexual initiative with her husband. Another friend is plagued with questions about her performance: Will she have an orgasm? Will she be a good lover for her husband?

Confidence is like a bank account. Each time we have a successful experience in any given endeavor—whether it is acquiring a new client at work or experiencing success at preparing yet another holiday dinner—we make a deposit in our confidence account. Even writing books falls under the dictates of this principle. At some point in the early weeks and months of *every* book I have ever written, I experience a confidence crisis. I clutch my breast and pull my hair and wail to my husband: "WHY in the world did I agree to write this book! I was such an IDIOT! I can't do this! I CAN'T DO THIS!" I've completed five

Intercourse bolsters hormones that maximize general good health.

books now, and I can honestly say that there has never been an exception. The good news is that with each successfully completed project, the balance in my confidence account grows. And as my balance grows, my fears decrease. With my earlier books, confidence crises lasted weeks . . . and then days . . . and now, merely hours.

To bolster your sexual confidence, set yourself up for a series of successful encounters. Don't sabotage yourself by initiating intimacy when, for whatever reasons, you run a higher risk of failure. Look frequently for moments when your environment and relationship with your husband are conducive to romance, then jump in. Take the chance. As soon as possible after one successful experience, go for another. Try not to let the good feelings from one passionate encounter fade too far into memory before initiating a repeat performance. As the momentum of passion and your growing confidence carry you along, I have no doubt that you'll be pleasantly surprised by the results.

Problem: "I'm Too Tired."
Solution: Do It for Your Energy Level.

There are few things in life that can deplete energy faster than good old-fashioned stress. And yet, according to Dr. Reed Moskowittz, founder and director of The Stress Disorders Medical Services at New York University Medical Center, there's nothing quite like lovemaking as a means of reducing stress. He says, "Sex is an antidote to the frustrations of civilized life. It lets our bodies regenerate and renew."

Sexual intimacy, orgasm in particular, creates a tremendous surge of adrenaline. Heartbeats race, muscles contract, and when the show is over, the body melts in delicious and total relaxation. Stress is erased.

Intercourse—and in some cases, cuddling without intercourse—also bolsters hormones that maximize general physical health. For example, studies show that women who make love at least once a week have higher levels of estrogen than women who don't. Among other things, estrogen lowers cholesterol, keeps the cardiovascular system running smoothly, makes our skin smoother, and helps prevent depression.

Frequent lovemaking also releases endorphins into our systems, which not only promotes an emotional sense of euphoria, but also results in increased levels of T cells, white blood cells vital for healthy immune systems. Finally, sex makes us more alert, stimulating circulatory and nervous systems.

You know, even the old standby excuse of having a headache falls by the wayside when we take a close look at the benefits of lovemaking. In one study, a majority of women reported that lovemaking actually *relieved the pain of migraine headaches.*

As far as I know, there may not be any really decent excuses for declining sexual intimacy with your spouse. Perhaps of them all, the only legitimate excuse that remains might be having to wash your hair. But if you want my advice, for smoother skin, more energy, fewer headaches, and a stronger heart, go ahead and spend the evening in the shower washing your hair. Just invite your husband along to help.

Jump In with Enthusiasm

A couple of weeks ago, Larry and I found ourselves sitting in a local pizza joint scarfing slices of greasy pepperoni pizza with buddies Dave and Diane. Our friends were excited to hear that I was launching another book project and asked eagerly about the topic of my newest endeavor. I told them it was an ABC book for women on sexuality. I described it, in fact, as sort of a primer for women who love sex.

Dave quipped: "Women who love sex? Oh! So it's a *fiction* book!"

We laughed. He was, after all, joking.

I think.

Yet the fact remains that many people stereotype women as disinterested in sex, while men are left to foam at the mouth in frustration and unrequited sexual desire.

Popular culture frequently portrays men as the pursuers and women as the party poopers . . . husbands as the initiators and wives as the cool guardians of the gates of passion.

Then again, is it all stereotype? Is it possible that you and I might actually buy into these roles now and then?

Do we leave the sexual pursuit too frequently to the men in our lives?

Do we invest more time and energy into clipping coupons than we do chasing our mates?

Could we . . . should we . . . show a little more enthusiasm when it comes to bedroom antics?

Everyone Wants to Be Wanted

One of my friends says that throughout her marriage she has tried to communicate to her husband the fact that, day or night, whenever he's in the mood for love, she's ready too. She enjoys sex and wants her husband to know that she welcomes his advances. I commend her for her attitude. This is, after all, a much healthier approach than communicating to your husband that to you sex is less of a priority than flossing your teeth or that you are only interested in lovemaking during lunar eclipses or appearances of Halley's Comet.

But I have to wonder. Is saying, "I'm happy when you want me" the same as communicating the message: "I want you"?

And who doesn't want to be wanted?

It's easy to tell ourselves that our husbands don't need the same kind of attention and strokes and nurturing that we want. Now, I'll be the first to agree that our *interpretations* of many needs are different—but beneath it all, our needs are not so diverse. *Everyone* wants to feel loved, appreciated, valued, and yes, physically and sexually desirable. It's true that the kinds of messages that best communicate to me that I am loved, appreciated, valued, or desirable may be *very* different from the messages that communicate these things to my husband. (You can read all about overcoming these kinds of "language barriers" to romance in chapter K.) And yet, beneath all the cultural, personality, and gender differences, many foundational similarities reside.

In other words, husbands need to feel sexy too. They want to know we want them . . . enjoy them . . . need them. It's important for them to know that the physical intimacy we share means as much to us as it does to them. They need to hear that they are handsome, that we find their bodies desirable, that they turn us on. They need to know that we are more than passive bystanders when it comes to sex—that we can, instead, muster actual *enthusiasm* for the lustier elements of marriage.

So How Do We Communicate Greater Enthusiasm?

There may be some women who have just read the previous paragraph and are even now muttering to themselves, "Oh, I get it. She wants me to *lie!*"

No, no. Lying is out. I certainly understand the fact that, particularly for women, the tides of passion ebb and flow. Monthly cycles, seasons of childbearing, the demands of a too-full schedule—all these things can dampen our enthusiasm for lovemaking. Yet even at moments when our enthusiasm is running low, I believe it is possible to find ways to sincerely and with integrity affirm the sexual desirability of the men we love. Here are some ideas:

1. Compliment physical features. Let's face it. We all can't be married to Tom Cruise look-a-likes. And yet the men we married possess physical features that, even if they are becoming blurred with age, attracted us in the beginning and very likely attract us still. My husband, for example, has sensual lips. When we were dating and then were newlyweds, I frequently told him that he had sexy lips and that his arms were sexy too. As I am writing this, however, I'm feeling somewhat convicted over the fact that, after fifteen years of marriage, I can't quite recall the last time I complimented his lips or his biceps. This is unfortunate, since I find him more handsome than ever, and I'm sure this is information that he would still enjoy hearing.

It's so easy to take each other for granted, isn't it? Are there compliments your husband hasn't heard in a while? Perhaps you can find an appropriate moment this week to pull a few out of the archives, dust them off, and share them with your husband.

2. Flirt with your husband. Remember the basics? Sure you do. Make lots of eye contact. Look for opportunities to touch his arm or hand or shoulder. Laugh warmly at his jokes. Lean toward him in undivided attention as he describes for you all the steps it took for him to jerry-rig the plumbing under the kitchen sink. When you greet him after work, do so with an arousing kiss. Spice up your evening conversation by admitting, "I missed you today," in a faintly suggestive tone. It shouldn't be too difficult; if you're like me, during your single years you expended more energy perfecting these kinds of skills than you did obtaining a college degree. If you are reviving them for the first time in years, you may feel a little rusty at first, but you should regain flirting fluency soon enough.

3. Find ways to tell your husband that you think making love is an enjoyable pastime. Whether you initiate a sexual encounter or your husband does, look for opportunities to verbalize your enthusiasm about the idea. As you snuggle and kiss, you might say something like, "I've been looking forward to this," or "I'm glad you suggested this—I've been missing you," or "This was a good idea."

One of my friends says she and her husband frequently make plans in the morning for lovemaking that night. The advance notice gives her time to mentally prepare and to budget her energy as she cares for three children throughout the day. She also uses this time to let her husband know she is looking forward to their "date." Sometimes she calls him at the office just to say she's thinking about the evening ahead. At other times she greets him at 5:30 with a quick kiss and whispered affirmation.

4. After the fact, refer to your lovemaking in a positive fashion. We already know that real life is not like the movies, where couples bask in the afterglow of lovemaking for eons. No, in real life we get to bask for entire nanoseconds until either partner falls asleep or pads barefoot to the bathroom. Yet even in this brief space of time there's an opportunity for an affirming comment: "Wow, that was great," "I really enjoy it when we make love," "Have I told you lately that you're a very sexy lover?"

Our comments don't even need to be confined to the moments following lovemaking. The morning-after provides another great chance to share our enthusiasm with our spouses. One morning as I was making oatmeal for breakfast, Larry came downstairs dressed for work, gave me a quick "good morning" hug, and said simply, "I enjoyed last night."

Kaitlyn, of course, wanted to know what it was she had missed: "Last night? What happened last night?"

I distracted her with the offer of chocolate chips to stir into her oatmeal, and the moment passed. What didn't fade, however, was the warm feeling I got from Larry's simple statement. It's a feeling the man in your life will enjoy as well. Ten minutes or ten hours after the fireworks have subsided, find a way to let him know that the memory of your lovemaking is still fresh and pleasant in your mind.

5. Initiate sex. When it comes to initiating sex, one woman I know is a wellspring of creative ideas. One day, for example, she spent her lunch hour shopping for clothing accessories for her husband. She bought suspenders, a belt, a tie clip, and a tie. That evening after dinner she announced to her husband, "I went shopping today and bought you some presents . . . but I've hidden them and it's up to you to find them!" She had, indeed, hidden the tie in her panties, tie clip in her bra, and was wearing the new belt and suspenders beneath her clothes. There is no question that with such a well-planned, creative approach this woman managed to communicate a sense of her enthusiasm to her happy husband!

Initiating lovemaking can be elaborate, or it can be executed with an impromptu touch or comment at bedtime after the kids are asleep. Either way, making the first move sends a welcome message to our husbands.

6. Make an investment of time or energy into your relationship with your husband. Doug Fields, author of the book *Creative Romance* (Harvest House, 1991), has compiled a list of "creative dating ideas" to encourage husbands and wives to invest wisely in the quality of their marriages. Many of his ideas, however, can also be used to communicate to your husband the fact that he is physically desirable to you and that you are excited about the intimacy you share with him. Here is a sampling:

- List your spouse's best qualities in alphabetical order.
- Notice the little changes your spouse makes in his appearance.
- Give your spouse a back rub.

- Remember to look into your spouse's eyes as he tells you about the day.
- Tell your spouse, "I'm glad I married you!"
- Send your spouse a love letter.
- Sit on the same side of a restaurant booth.
- Give your mate a foot massage.
- Tell your spouse, "I'd rather be here with you than any place in the world."
- Whisper something romantic to your spouse in a crowded room.
- Perfume the bedsheets.
- Serve breakfast in bed.
- Kiss in the rain.
- Brush his hair.
- Dedicate a song to him over the radio.
- Wink and smile at your spouse from across the room.
- Have a hot bubble bath ready for him at the end of a long day.
- Buy new satin sheets.
- Take time to think about him during the day, then share those thoughts.

7. Last but not least, ask your husband what communicates enthusiasm to him. My husband would say lingerie. Another husband might say he appreciates it when his wife makes the first move. A third might reveal that verbal affirmation makes him feel loved and desired. Your husband would say . . . who knows? Your best bet is to come right out and ask. In fact, the simple fact that you cared enough to raise the question will go far toward communicating to your husband that you are enthused about your love life together.

Kindle Romance

Let me tell you what I find romantic.

A bouquet of spring flowers. Steaks and candlelight. A gift of expensive cologne or a book I've been dying to read. Jewelry can be romantic; rings or earrings are my favorites. Water is always romantic: the pounding surf . . . playful nighttime swimming with the one you love . . . even taking a shower together. Doing nothing together can be romantic too; I love sitting in the swing or rocker on my porch and watching the world go by.

Larry and I were newlyweds when my twenty-second birthday rolled around. I remember him asking me what I wanted for my birthday. I thought a moment, mentally reviewing my list of favorite romantic things.

"Flowers would be nice," I suggested.

"Flowers?" Larry made a face. "They're not permanent. Pick something else. Something that won't end up standing dead in green water."

I went back to my mental list. "Okay, there's this list of books I've been dying to read. . . ."

Larry's eyebrows furrowed. "Books? Books are okay, but . . . well, I've been meaning to ask you about that. Have you considered using the library? You can read as much as you want, and it won't cost a dime."

"Library? LIBRARY?" I was mortified. "I'm a writer, Larry. I love books. Love the smell, the feel, the places they take me. Nix the library idea. I like to own my own books."

"Okay. But since I don't like to buy them, could you pick something else for your present?"

I sighed. "Maybe a piece of jewelry. . . ."

He shook his head. "I don't want to pick out jewelry. How would I know what you'd like? What else do you want?"

I don't remember how the conversation ended. Needless to say, it was not the birthday of my dreams. I had

Larry thinks camping is romantically bonding. I prefer room service.

my list of things that were meaningful to me, and while Larry's intent was to please me, he was trying to do so from *his* list, not mine.

I, on the other hand, made my share of similar mistakes.

I remember trying, in the early years of our marriage, to impress Larry with the kinds of attentive and romantic acts that I wanted to receive from him. There was, for example, the year when I planned a surprise birthday party for him, inviting everyone we knew, wanted to know, or had ever met briefly in passing. I was so excited—this was *exactly* the kind of thing I knew I would love to have done for me. Surely it would thrill Larry just as much.

He suffered through it. It seems I had never really taken into consideration the fact that my husband hates surprises and prefers small intimate gatherings to large groups.

Oh well.

Romance as a Foreign Language

Why is it so difficult to listen to our spouses—really listen—and to learn the language that speaks most directly to them? For years I simply assumed that the acts of kindness and romance that were so appealing to me would speak volumes to my husband. I sent message after message, never realizing that—like inserting a Macintosh disk into an IBM computer—my communiqués were simply not being read.

On the other hand, I felt bewildered by the lack of messages I was receiving from Larry. Where were the flowers and cards and verbal sweet-nothings that would fuel my fire? Little did I know that he was, indeed, sending messages of love, affirmation, and romance—unfortunately his messages, like mine, were going unread and unnoticed.

Do you want to kindle romance in your marriage? I wish I could offer you a one-hour course or some kind of overnight solution that would revolutionize your marriage. Unfortunately, kindling romance takes time and patience, and sometimes it means mastering a foreign language of love. If this seems easier said than done, it is. But perhaps we can simplify the process by looking at three steps to becoming bilingual in the languages of romance:

1. Learn the Language of Love

Kindling romance means learning to communicate your love to your husband in the terms he understands best, even if it is not your native tongue! What is your first step to learning the words and deeds that will communicate most directly to your husband? I believe the first step is to ask. That's right. It doesn't get much simpler than this, does it? Simply ask your husband to describe the acts—nonsexual and even sexual—that "say" something to him.

You might ask him to describe the things you do—or that he would *like* you to do—that have the power to

- comfort him
- turn him on sexually
- make him feel appreciated
- let him know that you respect him
- demonstrate the depth of your love for him

You might ask him to describe some of his fantasies—again, both sexual and nonsexual. Does he dream about world travel? Has he always wanted to ride in a hot-air balloon? Does he enjoy surprises, or does he prefer to plan and anticipate long-range? What kinds of activities or settings make him feel emotionally close to you?

Write down his answers. What you are compiling, of course, is a wish list of sorts. Some of the things on your husband's list may seem outrageous or unattainable. At the same time, you will also get many ideas that you can use as you try to tailor your words and actions to have the greatest impact on your husband—as you try to learn to "speak" the language he is most apt to hear.

While you are doing this, keep an open mind and DON'T CRITICIZE any of your husband's answers. You may think to yourself that your husband has better odds of winning the lottery than having some of his ideas come true, but try not to express this opinion to your husband via verbal or nonverbal communication. This means you are not allowed to roll your eyes, wince, or fall off your chair laughing hysterically.

Larry, for example, happens to think that camping is a romantically bonding experience. I, on the other hand, prefer room service. Larry says that it means a

If you've ever mastered a foreign language, you know that fluency takes time.

lot to him when I snuggle close and watch football games with him. I think that tight ends are best appreciated on the beach or in the gym, and that "sudden death" is a pretty good alternative to having to watch football on television.

But here's the thing: How badly do I want to communicate to him that I love him? How important is it to create the kinds of settings in which he feels emotionally close to me? How much do I want to speak the lingo that speaks most directly to him?

Oh well. *Monday Night Football*, here I come.

2. Recognize the Language of Love

This one's harder.

It's one thing, after all, to learn to speak the lingo your husband feels most comfortable with; it's another thing to learn to recognize what your husband is trying to tell you when he uses that same lingo to communicate to you.

There were many years when I thought Larry wasn't telling me he loved me. Larry, on the other hand, thought he was sending that message daily. He was, after all, meticulous about keeping my car tuned and oiled so that I would be safe while driving the freeways. He planned insurance policies and retirement funds so that I would be well cared for if anything happened to him. He was dedicated about doing the laundry whenever housework piled up in the face of one of my deadlines. He worked hard, he provided well for his family, he was faithful. Wasn't that enough? Wasn't I getting the message?

Actually, no.

I remember, after years of feeling slighted, making the decision to look for messages of love, Larry-style. It's true, there were no flowers, no poetic cards, no romantic surprises. But he was sending some sort of messages. The question was, could I learn to read them? Could I learn to appreciate them? Would they be enough?

Two things began to happen. The first thing that happened was that I began to see signs—different signs from

Your husband may be honestly unaware that back rubs unlock the door to your libido.

what I had been seeking for years, but signs nonetheless—of Larry's deep love for me. This still didn't light my romantic fires, but it made me feel better. Less resentful. Less defensive.

The second thing that happened was that I gained deeper insight into Larry's particular language of love. I began to see, in his pattern toward me, the way he wanted to be treated as well. Larry loves order. Did I want to make him feel loved and cared for? Simple. Keep the house clean and don't bounce any checks this month. Not my idea of romance, I'll tell you—but oddly enough, it speaks to him.

What are your husband's patterns? What messages is he sending your way? Can you begin to appreciate those messages? Do those messages give you any insights into ways you can better speak to him?

3. Teach the Language of Love

Ah, here's the good part. Unfortunately, this probably won't happen overnight. Teaching your language of love can take time. As in years.

You've asked your husband for his "wish list" and used it to tailor your words and deeds to meet his needs.

You've made an effort to recognize and affirm his gestures of love toward you, no matter how different they are from what you long for.

Now is the time to—gently, gently now—help your husband understand how he can better communicate his love to you. What words and deeds speak most directly to your heart?

Years ago I made a list and handed it to Larry. "These are the romantic things I'd like for you to do," I said.

Big mistake.

I don't think he appreciated my approach. The list went in a drawer somewhere and has yet to be reexposed to the light of day.

No, for us it took years of talking and negotiating and compromising. Occasional bold and heartfelt conversations were coupled with more informal hints and comments. Gradually my approach of "Here, do this," gave way to more tender explanations beginning with words such as, "Here's why _______ means so much to me."

Perhaps your husband is good with lists. Perhaps a list and a few reminders will do the trick. Maybe you'll need to take a more long-term approach. Regardless of your method, keep the following suggestions in mind:

- Don't be defensive. Avoid statements beginning with the words, "You never do (such and such) . . ."
- Do look for relaxed and intimate moments in which to broach the subject when your husband might be most open to your ideas.
- Don't let any one item on your "list" become a deal-breaker. Remember that your goal is to encourage your husband to communicate in words and actions that are meaningful to you. It's not necessary for him to fulfill everything on your wish list, just as you won't want to follow, verbatim, every item on his list.
- Do be direct, without being confrontational. Your husband may be honestly unaware of the fact that back rubs unlock the door to your libido or that you've always wanted to make love under the stars. Have you shared these insights with him? Or have you been hoping he would read your mind but feeling resentful when he doesn't?
- When possible, do explain what's in it for him. Rather than framing everything in terms of what he needs to do for you, help your husband understand that learning to speak your language will reap benefits for him as well. No one, after all, wants to have his or her messages of love returned unopened. Let your husband know that, if he wants to be truly effective in kindling romance and communicating his love to you, these are the kinds of

words and deeds that will allow him to best achieve his goals.

Fluency Takes Time

If you've ever mastered a foreign language, you know that fluency takes time. It can take years. It can even take a lifetime. Kindling romance in your marriage requires nothing less. It is the lifelong pursuit of becoming bilingual in the languages of love.

And yet the rewards are great.

I happen to be writing this chapter on February 13th, a few hours before Valentine's Day. Looking through my office door, I can peer into my kitchen and glimpse a heartwarming sight. On my kitchen table blooms a bouquet of a dozen pink roses. They arrived a day early, unsolicited, a surprise from my husband. And with the gift comes a message made even more precious because it was communicated in my husband's "second language," a language he's learning for me and me alone.

We've come a long way, he and I. And we're still learning. Best yet, if we can do it, I know you can too.

Make the effort. Take the time. Learn his language. Teach him yours. Practice patience, be diligent, have faith. You, too, can become bilingual in the languages of the heart.

Lighten Up

Last month I bought a desk calendar by cartoonist Gary Larson—you know, the kind with a page for every day of the year. It's November now, so it won't be good for another couple of months. Actually, the calendar may never be usable—as a calendar that is—even when January arrives. This is because I can't keep my hands off it. I flip through it frequently, laughing at the cartoons revealing Larson's quick wit and skewed perspectives on life. In fact, I have already torn out several pages containing favorite cartoons and mailed or faxed them to friends. By the time January arrives, I'm not going to have much use for a 117-day calendar.

We love to laugh, don't we? Humor eases tension. It diffuses embarrassment. It enlarges our perspective. Smiling frequently reduces the odds of developing unwanted wrinkles in our faces (I am not making this up). Even the Bible tells us that a cheerful heart is good medicine.

Why not bring some of the magic, healing power of humor into our bedrooms? There is, after all, a place for frivolity in almost every other arena of life.

Sex is no different. It can be passionate. It can be poignant. But it can also be a whole lot of fun.

Laughter Helps Us Cope

There are plenty of reasons laughter has a place in the bedroom.

For starters, humor is a wonderful resource when it comes to coping with some of life's more awkward moments. And since sexuality thrives best in an atmosphere of vulnerability and transparency, there are plenty of opportunities for awkward moments to occur. If we're feeling shy, embarrassed, vulnerable, laughter can ease the moment. Unlike the movies, sex in real life is flawed and imperfect and very, very human; sometimes the very best response is simply to shrug and smile and learn to appreciate the lighter side of lovemaking.

Take Jim and Nanette for example. Married for eight years, Jim and Nanette loved kids and hoped to begin a family soon. In the meantime, they were active in ministry to children and youth in their church, helping out where they could. One year they agreed to help chaperone their church's winter youth camp. The offer was readily accepted, and Jim and Nanette were assigned to a cabin of eight high school girls.

On the afternoon of the third day of camp, the girls left the cabin to throw snowballs at some of the boys from an adjacent cabin, and Jim and Nan found themselves alone for the first time in several days. Sitting together on the couch in a cozy cabin on a snowcapped mountain, they began the kind of romantic interchange that is so common among couples in love.

Nan said, "I took my temperature this morning and I'm ovulating."

Jim groaned. "Oh, fine. Here we are in a mountain cabin chaperoning eight high school girls. How are we supposed to have sex?"

Nan shrugged. "We could do it now. They're all outside."

"Yeah right. What if one of them comes back early?"

Nan giggled. "Some chaperones we'd turn out to be, huh?"

"Besides, my back still aches. Those cots are not exactly orthopedic quality. Are you really in the mood?"

"No. But it's not like it takes an hour. Three minutes, tops."

"Maybe you're right. I guess we could hurry before anyone gets back."

About that time, their conversation was interrupted by a quick rap on the cabin door. The door creaked open and revealed the head of a sophomore boy. He said, "Hi, 'scuse me, I'm looking for Jennifer."

Jim answered. "She's not here. They're all outside throwing snowballs."

"Oh. I was supposed to meet her here."

"Sorry. She left with the others."

The boy was about to leave when a small voice piped up from the loft immediately above Jim and Nan's heads. Jennifer, in a voice both timid and blushing, said simply, "Wait. I'm up here."

You can scream. You can cry.

Or you can wince and grin, shrug and smile, and learn to laugh at the flaws and foibles of life and love.

Laughter Provides Transition

It took Larry and me too long to learn that laughter can help us transition from one emotional state to another. There was a time, fairly early in our marriage, when we were in a rut. We were experiencing the normal squabbles inherent in every marriage. We just hadn't found a good way to transition ourselves out of the tension of our disagreements and back into harmony. Our quickest transition seemed to be two days of cool greetings, cold shoulders, and colder nights. Believe me when I tell you that this pattern was not particularly conducive to marital harmony.

Eventually we began looking for alternatives. The best to date—and I have to give my husband full credit for initiating this new policy—is laughter.

There are simply times when we are both a little grouchy, picking at each other and teetering on the edge of falling into real tension over nothing in particular, and Larry will suddenly say or do something exaggerated, outrageous, or even corny and make me laugh. Once that happens, it's over. The tension's gone, the perilous moment has passed, and we're friends again.

Oh, how potent is a smile, to transport us suddenly from one world into another! Just as laughter can transition us into marital harmony or out of the clutches of a stress-filled day, it can also provide a wonderful transition into sexual intimacy. Now, I'm assuming you realize I'm not talking about guffawing at your husband's skinny legs or telling jokes that start, "How many balding middle-aged men does it take to change a lightbulb?"

Laughing *at* your spouse will provide some sort of transition, but probably not to anywhere you'd like to go. No, I'm talking about something else entirely.

In the early years of their marriage, Stanley and Carol decided they needed some sort of transition to take them from the rigors of family life into the intimacy shared by husband and wife. This was crucial for them since these

I'm assuming you realize I'm not talking about guffawing at your husband's skinny legs.

newlyweds were facing new stepparenting challenges as Carol became, in one fell swoop, wife to Stanley and mother to his children by a previous marriage.

Each evening they began this transition by putting the kids to bed and retiring early to their own bedroom. There they took several moments to light upwards of forty candles that Carol had purchased and scattered around the room. They spent the next hour relaxing and reading favorite books by candlelight. And then the fun began.

The trick was to take turns blowing out the forty-some candles—while being tickled by your spouse. Taking turns, they would submit themselves to the indignities of being tickled while trying to catch a breath long enough to blow out candles. Laughing and blowing are, of course, mutually exclusive endeavors. Sometimes the process ended with the couple collapsed in laughter on the bed; frequently it ended in romance.

Laughter. What a gift! It can help us cope. It can create a segue from one emotional place to another. Finally, it can help provide a silver chord of connection between friends and lovers.

Laughter Builds a Bond

Funny pet names. Inside jokes. Comic rituals. Silly secrets. These are the private endearments that enrich our relationships and help forge lasting bonds between individuals. Sometimes the private humor between friends is more potent when it is kept from outsiders—at other times, well . . . it can't be shared no matter how hard we try!

Take my sister and me, for example. When Michelle and I are together, there are moments all my husband can do is shake his head in disbelief. He somehow finds it incredible that we could dissolve into hysterical laughter over simple phrases such as "The Italian Hair" or "Burn, Cookie, Burn!" Sometimes I try to explain our inside jokes to him—like Michelle's Scooby-Doo-Cartoon-Dash-out-of-the-Texas-Hailstorm—but they seem to lose something in the retelling. I guess sometimes you just had to have been there.

The same kind of bonding takes place when lovers laugh together. Something is created. Something that can't be shared. Something that belongs to you and your husband and no one else.

For example, one of my friends admitted that, one night, her husband named her breasts. The left one is Sam and the right George. Of course, I asked her why—of all the names in the world—he chose Sam and George. But she wouldn't say. She was laughing too hard at whatever private joke she shares with her husband that evoked the names in the first place.

Pet names. Inside jokes. Comic rituals. Silly secrets. They have a place in our lives in other arenas, with other people. If we let it, that same kind of good-natured humor can enrich our intimate moments with our spouses as well!

Make Time to Make Love

Recently Kaitlyn made an interesting observation. We were sitting in a rocking chair on our front porch, her hand on my protruding belly, talking about advice she'd like to give the new brother or sister who was still several months away from birth. One of the things she plans to say to our new baby is that, of the first eight years of life (which is the particular segment of time Kaitlyn can discuss firsthand), the very best age happens to be three.

When I asked Kaitlyn why being three was better than being eight, she rolled her eyes and breathed an exasperated sigh as if I should know.

"When you're eight you have too many *responsibilities,*" she said.

Too many responsibilities. Where does she get this stuff? No, wait, I know. Just yesterday my husband was complaining about having no free time. Kaitlyn was sitting in the room, absorbing every word. When he was through, she looked at him and nodded sympathetically. "I know what you mean," she agreed. "I don't have any free time either." When Larry looked surprised, Kaitlyn explained, "I'm doing something EVERY minute, Dad! There's school, homework, ballet, piano, roller skating, playing Barbies, watching cartoons, feeding Moonshine, playing house, playing computer games, coloring, reading books . . ."

Oh, the leisurely life of a child. You and I can smile, because we know what responsibility really is. It's mortgages and car pools and overdue bills and signing up for one too many PTA committees. It's working long hours on the job and longer hours once you finally get home at night. It's falling into bed too tired to change your clothes. It's never having enough time to wash your hair *and* shave your legs during the same shower.

When my friend Cherie describes her hectic schedule, she doesn't lament her lack of free time; she bemoans the lack of time available for some of life's most basic requests. She explains, "Some days I have to go to the bathroom so bad, but there's not a moment to spare. I'm running car pools, getting snacks, supervising homework, making dinner. When I finally get a minute and head down the hall, little voices follow me even then. I find myself shouting through the locked door, 'I have to go potty! Can't I have a single minute to myself JUST TO GO POTTY?'"

Talk about no free time!

It doesn't come as a big surprise that all this grown-up responsibility and lack of free time might, in some way, begin to infringe on our intimate moments with our husbands. Who among us would not agree with the statement that, given more free time, we could:

a. be more spontaneous lovers
b. have more energy at bedtime

c. put more effort into planning romantic surprises for our husbands
d. look like Cindy Crawford
e. all of the above

I'll admit that you and I are busy. Time is an issue. We face valid, nonstop demands during the majority of hours in our days. By the time evening rolls around, we're virtually brain-dead. There are simply some nights we crawl

Once we found romance in the backseat. Now romance takes a backseat to everything else in our lives.

into bed feeling more like roadkill than romantic. We are not joking when we tell our husbands that we'll agree to sex only if they promise not to wake us in the process.

On the one hand, we are completely justified. There really isn't enough time in the day to be all things to all people. When we were young and carefree, we found romance *in* the backseat. Nowadays, it seems as though romance has to *take* a backseat to every other demand, need, and responsibility in our busy lives.

And yet—listen carefully here even though you may not like what I'm about to say—we somehow manage to find time for the things we really want to do, don't we?

Last year I wrote a book for parents who want to become more involved in spiritual warfare for their children. In one of the chapters I talked about priorities as they pertained to our prayer lives, suggesting that we waste enough time each day on trivial, mindless pursuits that, with a little redirection of our time, we could find plenty of moments for prayer.

One of the observations I made was simply this: Did you know that in your lifetime, if you are like the average adult, you will be able to look back on your years on earth and realize that you spent an accumulated total of *three years* . . . are you ready? . . . Drum roll, please . . .

a total of three years . . .

watching television . . .

COMMERCIALS!

That's right. I'm not talking about spending three years watching the 6:00 news or the movie of the week. I'm talking about spending three years with the Energizer Bunny. I mean, if I can make time for the Energizer Bunny, you'd think I could carve out a few moments now and then for the father of my children.

Even in the most hurried and harried schedules, is it possible to find time for the things that really matter to us?

I believe it is.

I've had women approach me and say wistfully, "I'd really love to be a writer, but I just don't have any time."

About that time I usually want to launch into my personal testimony about the scheduling hardships that I faced while writing my first books. It's one of those "I wrote books barefoot in the snow uphill both ways" kind of stories that makes the listener smile politely and wish she was somewhere else. Anywhere else. Like getting a root canal or something.

Of course you realize that after saying all that, I am obligated to go ahead and tell the story, don't you? Hang on to your molars; I'll try to make it brief.

I wrote my first book while holding down a full-time job, writing before work, after work, and in the middle of the night.

I wrote my second book at home with a newborn baby while holding down a part-time job. I wrote in the early mornings, late at night, and in those really quiet hours just before dawn would break and my precious darling infant with the pink rosebud lips would wake from her slumber, ponder the desirability of a warm breakfast, then signal me of her intentions by screaming like a fire-truck siren.

I have a passion for writing. And I find the time. Weird niches of time when the rest of the world is asleep, but I find the time. On the other hand, I am decidedly passionless about housekeeping. And guess what? I never have time to finish the laundry. Never. So I ask you: Is this a mere dilemma in time management?

I think not.

(Okay. Story's over.)

The bottom line is this: We make time for the things for which we have a passion. Sometimes it takes effort and planning and the sacrifice of lesser goods in order to achieve something on which we've set our sights. But it's possible.

This principle applies to writing books.

As much as I hate to admit it, this principle also applies to housework.

Finally, this principle applies to sex. The "No Time for Sex or Romance" excuse might work for a night. Or a week or two. But not for months and certainly not for the life of a marriage. Because it will attempt to do so, you know. Our schedules don't prune themselves. If we regularly allow the routine in our lives to choke out the romance, the habit will become a difficult one to break. It will undermine our marriages unless, wielding machetes and industrial-strength pruning shears, we wade into the tangled growth of overcommitments and out-of-balance priorities.

We *can* carve out time for love.

But it has to be something we really want to do.

Do We *Want* to Make Time for Love?

Ann has been complaining for eleven years about her unsatisfactory sex life. To hear Ann's side of the story, you would think that she has been ready and willing for more than a decade, while her husband has all the hang-ups.

Lately she's come to the realization that her story accurately describes only the first half of her marriage. During the second half of her marriage, Ann was not as ready and willing as she likes to remember; in reality, she began to withdraw her sexuality into a protective shell. For the past five years, Ann has been sending subtle and not so subtle "keep away" messages to her husband. She says she wants a sexier marriage—but her actions tell a different story.

There are myriad reasons for a woman to decide she *does not want* a more intimate sex life with her husband. These reasons might include fear of rejection, unresolved anger toward a husband or even toward a parent, a past trauma such as molestation or rape, beleaguered self-esteem, broken trust due to a husband's infidelity, a growing attraction to—or even an affair with—another man, the hardening of a protective shell against the wounds and bruises of an emotionally or physically abusive marriage, or insecurities about her physical appearance and attractiveness. And the list could go on and on.

I know that in my life, when I find myself—over a significant period of time—justifying a less-than-ideal love life by placing the blame squarely on schedules or fatigue or on something my husband is or is not doing, it usually means I'm overlooking a key element. During these excuse-laden moments, if I really want to identify the dominant party pooper, I'd do well to walk into the bathroom and greet the face in the mirror.

What about you? Do you give lip service to the concept that you wish you had more time for romance with your husband? Of course, it is inevitable that there will be days and weeks when harried schedules hinder heavy breathing in the bedroom. But in the long run . . . well, actions speak louder than words. You say you desire greater sexual intimacy with your husband. Do your actions support your words? Or do they tell a different story?

When Ann told me about her growing realization that regardless of her words she really hadn't *wanted* to experience greater intimacy with Bill, I asked her how she had begun to clue in to her deeper feelings. What were the signs, the actions that had finally spoken loudest of all?

Ann talked about gaining twenty pounds, working longer hours at her office and spending less time at home, retiring to the bedroom long before she knew her husband would be ready to come to bed, abandoning her prettier gowns for sleepwear that was long on function and short on fashion, sleeping closer to the wall than to her husband, and spending less time and energy on her appearance during evenings and weekends when she knew she and Bill would spend the most time together.

Other women I've talked to have mentioned decreasing eye-contact with their husbands, avoiding even nonsexual touch like holding hands or sitting close on the couch, and avoiding intimate topics of conversation that would leave them emotionally vulnerable or transparent.

If any of these actions mirror behaviors in your own life, time management is not your answer. You may have deeper issues to examine before the clock in your bedroom will ever signify adequate time for lovemaking.

Do you want to make more time for love? If you have been sabotaging your own desires with subtle "keep away" messages, the answer is probably no. But don't be discouraged: You can turn that no into a resounding yes! Here are a few suggestions on how to go about it:

You deserve the truth. Be honest with yourself. Don't use busy schedules or fatigue or even your children as an excuse to avoid something you're not sure you want to do anyway.

Exchange excuses for solutions. If you determine that you are, for whatever reason, avoiding sexual intimacy, work at resolving the conflict that is holding you back. Perhaps the simple realization that you are being bound by a festering grudge, for example, will be enough to allow you to let go of your anger and renew your commitment to sexual and emotional intimacy with your husband. If the problem is more complicated, then more proactive steps might be necessary. Fasting and prayer, accountability with a friend, or Christian counseling are options you may want to consider.

Schedule time for romance. With foundational issues out of the way, you are truly ready to tackle the smaller, nagging annoyances like synchronizing harried and headlong schedules. It can be done. Make a steady investment of time into your marriage and you will reap dividends for decades to come.

There's no magic formula to finding the time you need to cultivate a satisfying and thriving love life with your husband. It's as simple as remembering that we find time for things for which we have a passion. As they say, where there's a will, there's a way. All we need is the passion and the will. The time will follow.

Navigate Troubled Waters

I remember the first time I cruised a river in an inner tube. I was sixteen and far more concerned about what river spray would do to my mascara than I was about the rocks and rapids that awaited me downstream.

Five years later, I took much the same approach to marriage. *Rocks? Rapids? Turbulence? My marriage? You've got to be joking!* To make matters worse, the first time Larry and I cruised into troubled waters, I looked around and made a rash assumption. I saw other couples around us navigating their marriages with apparent ease, and I assumed that their love lives were idyllic. I was certain that no one else had ever faced the same rough waters Larry and I were facing. I felt panic. I felt alone. I felt hopeless. And I was certain the problems we were facing were unique in all the earth.

I know now that I was wrong.

Every marriage has its share of troubled waters. They might occur during the first week of matrimony or the thousandth. They can roil around us for very obvious reasons, or for no apparent reason at all. They occur the first time we consider our love lives with our husbands and acknowledge that, well, things could be better.

Troubled waters might be caused by disillusionment. Or boredom. Or the arrival of children who, like small diapered aliens from another planet, siphon the very strength from our bodies and use it to keep their own bodies energized, wailing and flailing, until three in the morning.

Troubled waters might be caused by simple incongruencies between your vision of ideal sex and your husband's, something as simple as that the positions you enjoy, the frequency you desire, and the transitions you require are vastly different from what he enjoys, desires, and requires.

Or they might be brought about by something as complex as the gradual and steady construction of a stone wall between you and your husband, a wall carefully hewn from a vast quarry of inflicted hurts and unresolved anger.

Troubled waters may even be the result of some conflict, habit, or wound from before your marriage, such as:

- memories of an ex-spouse
- the delayed emotional impact of childhood abuse
- the lingering and seductive fingers of premarital promiscuity
- the hard-to-shake dregs of some misdirected childhood teaching such as the concept that sex is dirty,
- or that it is a woman's duty to live in sexual submission to her husband
- or perhaps that somewhere in some part of the Bible that everyone knows about but that no one can ac-

tually point to it says that Christians aren't supposed to really enjoy the act of lovemaking, but are simply to put up with it for purposes of procreation

Finally, perhaps there is something about the "performance" of your bodies during lovemaking that is gradually eroding the joy from your love life, such as impotence or premature ejaculation for a man, or infrequent orgasms for a woman. Maybe it is the small sacrifices demanded by aging bodies, or the abrupt intrusion of an illness or disability that threatens to redefine your sexuality and perhaps even your marriage.

Regardless of the source, there are moments in every marriage when all is not smooth sailing in the bedroom. Rocks and waves threaten to capsize your relationship at every turn. The Love Boat is taking on water, folks, and not even Captain Stubing can save you now.

Information Island

When we are floundering in the turbulent sea of love, accurate and practical information can provide a welcome foundation from which to enhance, help, and even heal our love lives.

After all, in every other arena of marriage, we can find an abundance of information to help us through the flaws, foibles, and adjustments of everyday living. For example, is my problem a lack of culinary talent? If so, I can take a cooking class, watch cooking lessons on cable TV, or ask a friend for a recipe.

Is my problem a colicky baby or diaper rash? Any woman toting a diaper bag or stocking up on Gerber peas and carrots on grocery aisle 9 would be more than happy to stop and answer my questions.

Is my problem a lack of organization in my kitchen cupboards? I can always ask Heloise.

Is my problem the fact that I'm not sure I've ever had an orgasm? Or that my husband wants sex nine times a week? Or that he can't maintain an erection? Or that I experience pain during intercourse? I may wonder if my friends or neighbors have ever had a similar experience, and if so, I may be desperate to know what they did about the problem. But it's just not the kind of thing you bring up across the backyard fence or while negotiating who's driving the car pool next week.

And yet, I believe that the majority of disillusionments in the bedroom are simply the result of a lack of information.

For example, if your husband ejaculates too quickly to enable you to experience an orgasm of your own, there are simple exercises he can do alone and that you both can do together, which may well enable him to maintain an erection longer and delay ejaculation.

Did you know that a perceived inability to experience orgasm is one of the most common complaints women make? And yet there are solutions. For example, studies have shown that twenty minutes of foreplay can enable many women to experience orgasm, and yet most couples engage in foreplay for less than fifteen minutes. Achieving orgasm may be as simple as prolonging foreplay, teaching your husband new ways to stimulate you, or negotiating better transitions from your role as employee/homemaker/mother/etc. to your role as lover.

Making love, like any other skill, needs to be learned. Good sexual technique is not picked up by osmosis. Understanding gender differences in general and the unique needs and desires of your spouse in specific is not instinctual. These things must be learned. And learning takes time. And information.

Unfortunately, we get a lot of our ideas about sex from the media magicians who seem determined to create highly unrealistic and implausible caricatures of real life and flaunt them in TV movies, commercials, magazines, novels, billboards, and the silver screen.

For accurate information regarding our sexuality, we're better off to attend a marriage seminar, broach the subject with a physician, talk to a trusted friend who may have traveled a little farther down the road of life and marriage than we have, or browse a self-help book written by a credible source. *Restoring the Pleasure* (Word, 1993), for example, is an excellent resource for couples seeking detailed explanations and information regarding their sexuality. Written by Christian sex therapists Joyce and Cliff Penner, the book is touted as containing "complete step-by-step programs to help couples overcome the most common sexual barriers." Indeed, it presents exercises designed to help couples overcome an array of barriers to a satisfying sex life, including the ejaculation and orgasm problems mentioned above.

Finally, there are two other profound sources of invaluable information that will enhance your sex life:

1. You.
2. Your husband.

You know more about your sexual needs—what works and what doesn't work for you—than anyone else. Your husband NEEDS that information. You, on the other hand, need to know what he's thinking and feeling as well. Patricia Love, quoted earlier as the author of the book *Hot Monogamy,* writes, "My clients pay me good money to paraphrase what their partners have been telling them for years." Learn to listen to the "experts" in your own bedroom. You and your husband may very well hold the secrets to improving your love life. Talk to each other. Listen to each other.

Mayday . . . Mayday . . . Radioing for Professional Help

It would be nice if every bedroom dilemma could be dissolved with a dose of well-placed knowledge. Sometimes, however, it takes process, not information, to help a couple slowly wend their way back into still and peaceful marital waters.

One friend of mine, for example, is slowly coming to the realization that she can no longer deny the impact of childhood molestation on her marriage. For nearly a decade she has fought to ignore bedroom tensions and sexual barriers stemming from tragic events that occurred during her childhood. Unfortunately, the psychological and emotional ramifications of sexual abuse will not dissipate with the simple knowledge that orgasm may be twenty minutes away or that Kegel exercises can enhance sexual pleasure. No, the solution to Erin's dilemma may well lie in months—maybe even several years—of wise and tender guidance from a Christian therapist, pastor, or counselor.

Regardless of the resource that meets the needs of you and your husband—seminars, books, therapy, lay counseling, medical advice, or improved communication—the first necessary step is to care enough about your marriage to seek a solution to the barriers that are robbing you of sexual intimacy. Don't be embarrassed to ask for help; successful marriages, after all, are not the result of problem-free relationships (which are, by the way, about as statistically common as leprechauns). Instead, successful, rewarding marriages are the result of hard work by committed couples who know how to get the help they need *when* (notice I didn't say *if*) problems occur.

Overcome Poor Body Image

You can't say that Providence doesn't have a sense of humor. When I originated the outline for this book over a year ago, I had no idea that my deadline countdown and reproductive schedule would conspire to have me writing a chapter on body image while eight-and-a-half months pregnant.

Body image? To get a clear image of *my* body I'd do well to go downtown and peer into the side of one of those mirrored skyscrapers; my two-by-three-foot bathroom mirror just isn't big enough anymore.

Luckily for me and maybe even for you, this chapter isn't about how our bodies look. It's about how we feel about our bodies. Maybe a better title for this chapter would be "Improve Your Body Attitude." But then, of course, I'd be stuck with an orphaned letter *O*.

Body image is about confidence. It's about having a mental picture of yourself that generates positive feelings. How do you know if you have a good body image? If you'd rather undergo a root canal than catch a glimpse of yourself naked in a full-length mirror, read on. (On the other hand, if you can make love with all the lights on without the slightest reservation, maybe you should be the one writing this chapter.)

Having said all that, let's talk body image. I went through my phone book yesterday and spent the afternoon interviewing women I know. (It *had* to be women I know. Only a friend would submit herself to the indignities of being interrogated about body image. This is, by the way, how I get rid of those annoying dinner-time sales calls: "Sure, I'll answer your questions about my need for vinyl siding if you'll let me interview you for the book I'm writing on sex . . . Hello? . . . *Hello?*")

I wish I could say that in the process I had located a woman, any woman, who wasn't willing to trade in one or more body parts for something a little smaller, perkier, shinier, less wrinkled. According to my "research," it seems we're all in agreement: We all yearn to walk into our prayer closets, identify an ill-fitting item and say, "Excuse me, God, could I see this in a size eight?"

During my teens and twenties, I lamented the size of my nose. With the exception of my nose, I was certain I was near perfection. Ten years later, I'd still like to lose a quarter pound from my nose . . . plus another forty-nine and three quarters from the rest of my body. My friend Nancy pines for thicker hair and thinner hips; Cheryl refuses to wear sandals because she hates the look of her feet; my sister Michelle once sat at my kitchen table and shed tears over her wrinkled thumbs.

Of course, we've all heard the idiom that no one's perfect, physically or otherwise. Intellectually, we know this is a fairly accurate assessment of humanity. Emotionally, however, you may feel like I do; I'm convinced that if there aren't any perfect bodies, there should be, and there's no earthly reason why one of them shouldn't be mine.

Even actresses and models aren't immune from the laws and flaws of nature. I remember the day, several years ago, when I first learned about the existence of "body part" models. These are men and women who

Flawless women are about as commonplace as tooth fairies.

make a living modeling segments of their anatomy as "stand ins" for actors and actresses. Here's how it works. Let's say your favorite actress is in a scene requiring a close-up shot of her hands. It's entirely feasible that the flawless digits you see on your TV screen are not those of Julia Roberts at all, but the pampered palms of a hand model. And it's not just hands. Thighs, breasts, and even derrieres are also up for grabs (figuratively speaking).

I don't know how you feel about this particular facet of Hollywood trickery, but it made me angry. For years I've been comparing myself unfavorably to the flickering images of flawless womanhood on the silver screen only to find out that these icons of perfection, quite simply, DO NOT EXIST. Even all the moneybags and power moguls of Hollywood cannot locate in a single woman all of the "best" physical amenities. So what do they do? They create a celluloid composite of the choicest features and present them to society as the ideal woman. Of course, no one bothers to let us in on the secret that the hottest new starlet has wrinkled hands and the hand model has Hindenburg hips. You and I only get to view (and compare ourselves to) the finished product: the perfect woman.

Frankenstein would be proud.

Wanted: Great Body Image. Great Body Not Required.

If developing a good body image required a perfect body, we'd all be in trouble. No, flawless women are about as commonplace as unicorns or tooth fairies. And as for the women who come a little closer to perfection than the rest of us, well, the stories of drop-dead gorgeous women crippled by insecurities, obsessions, or eating disorders are so common they have become nearly cliché.

So what's the answer? If a great body is not the most important component in developing a great body image, then what is? How can we cast off our insecurities and become more confident about the skins in which we live?

I am not an "expert" on this subject. By this, I mean that I cannot stand before you honestly and tell you that I am happy, confident, and content with every aspect of my body. I am, in fact, a veteran of the body image wars just as you are. I, too, have fought the battle of the bulge and lost. I, too, have been ambushed by unsightly facial hairs. My arsenal, like yours, contains an array of bottles, formulas, and potions that, if marketing claims were gospel, contain the transforming powers to erase the uglies from an orangutan.

Then again, maybe that's okay. If I were perfect, you wouldn't trust me—you know it's true. And if I were perfect *and* confident about myself to boot, you'd be fighting the constant urge to have me arrested by some third world militia and shot at dawn.

So. From one imperfect, insecure person to another, how do we do it? How can we forgive ourselves our flaws and get on with the business of loving and enjoying the bodies we've been given?

Here are a few suggestions. To make them easier to remember, I've arranged them acrostically. Take the first letter of each key word, put them together, and they spell PPPPP. Hard to pronounce, but equally hard to misspell. And hopefully easy to remember. So here they are: The Five *P*s of Developing a Better Body Image.

1. Perspective

Like many of us, my friend Jackie would like to lose thirty pounds. For one thing, the added weight robs her of energy. For another, she says it's harder to feel sexy. Oh, her husband has never complained, but Jackie spends a good part of their lovemaking feeling more embarrassed than aroused.

Several months ago, while helping her twelve-year-old daughter with a homework assignment, Jackie gained a new perspective that culminated in renewed fervor in the bedroom. Jackie explains:

"Melissa was doing a research paper on the seventeenth-century painter Paul Rubens. He's famous for painting naked, buxom, glowing women of the Renaissance. Buxom, in fact, might be putting it mildly. As Melissa and I were going through a library book filled with photos of his paintings, it struck me that the women he painted—considered beautiful in his day and in ours as well—were fat. They had thunder thighs and thick waists and rolling bosoms and they were sensuous and confident and beautiful. The more I looked at his work, the more I began to think about myself. Maybe I could be sensuous and confident and beautiful too."

That night she had an opportunity to put her hypothesis to the test. She reports that she was less inhibited and more adventurous than she had been in years. After the fireworks, her husband—exhausted, spent, and happy—summed up the evening with a simple "Wow."

Later, curled in the crook of her husband's arm, Jackie talked about the events that gave her a new perspective and helped her begin to accept her body with all of its voluptuous stuffing and comfortable curves. When she was through, her husband kissed her tenderly on the top of her head and said, "Maybe you should help Melissa with her homework more often."

Does Jackie still need to lose thirty pounds? For her physical health, yes. Does she need to lose thirty pounds before she can feel pretty and sexy and confident? No. Can you and I develop a new perspective on our bodies, as imperfect as they may be? YES! Here are some ideas:

- What the heck—check out an art book from your local library and take a gander at the chunky beauties who, through the centuries, have attracted the eye of artists and painters.
- Lighten up—not your weight, but your attitude. Don't take your imperfections so seriously. If your nemesis is your bathroom scale, you might find some humor in the bumper-sticker slogan I saw recently on the road: "I might be fat, but you're ugly, and I can diet!"
- While reading magazines, watch for confessions from the "beautiful people" that give glimpses behind the facade and into their real worlds. My favorite is the one I found in a *People* magazine interview with Courtney Cox. The actress and former girlfriend of Michael Keaton had this to say about herself: "I can still hear my brother Richard's voice. We'd be riding

in his pickup, and he'd turn to me and say, 'Gee whiz, Cece, what's that hair growing out of your chin?' You don't think I get up and check my nose hairs every morning?" Clip photos of actors and actresses caught on a bad hair day. Remind yourself frequently that WE ALL share the human condition. You are not a second-class citizen because your hands sweat or you have morning breath, or you've gained a few pounds. Believe it or not, Diane Sawyer has morning breath, and Vanna White knows how to spell flatulence. So don't be so hard on yourself.

2. Priorities

I once met a woman who bragged she still had pert, firm breasts after nursing four babies. She was in her forties, with large, workworn hands and prematurely gray hair that she pulled back into a loose ponytail while she worked.

A seamstress, she ran a small business from her dining-room table, and we met while I was being fitted for a bridesmaid dress for my sister's wedding. Held captive in twenty-seven yards of velvet mined with straight pins, I learned more about this woman's milk wagons than anybody ought to have to know.

Four babies? Perky breasts? It's not that I don't believe her, but . . . if she told me the sun was shining in July I'd want a second opinion. At the time of our conversation, Kaitlyn was two years old. I had nursed her until she was fifteen months old and the last time my breasts had "perked" I was at Knott's Berry Farm riding the Parachute Drop. (You can get almost anything to perk if you strap yourself into a wire cage six stories high and free fall toward earth at something approximating the speed of light.)

Some things just take a toll on the ol' body. I wish there were an alternative, but there's not. Carrying, bearing, and nursing babies exacts a heavy duty in stretch marks, widened hips, and tired breasts. Caring for a young family can mean dark circles from sleepless nights, dishpan hands, and a permanent squint from driving into the sun as you carpool fourteen hours a week. Raising teenagers? Say hello to worry wrinkles above your brow, premature gray, and arthritic fingers from having to spend eight years gripping your wallet tightly in a futile, protective gesture.

A few days ago I took a long look at my hands. I was a little surprised to see that the smooth, taut skin of my youth had been replaced; I have the hands of a mom, a housewife, a woman closer to forty than thirty. I was a little sad, but not very. Yes, I have the hands of a woman. I also have a home and a family and a career and a dog. I have things to do and people to love. I have a history. I've lived an estimated half of my life on this earth, and I've got the scars and the laugh lines to prove it.

The old line "age before beauty" says something about the value of experience and age versus the value of mere beauty. Don't begrudge someone her youthful looks—instead, learn to appreciate, respect, and even cherish the small sacrifices that are required of your body by the passage of time.

3. Practice Habits that Boost Your Confidence

I used to think that diet and exercise were about weight and looks. Now I know better. The primary benefits are *not* reduced weight and a streamlined shape, although those can certainly be by-products of a consistent regimen.

When I was dieting and exercising solely to improve my looks, I frequently became discouraged. I'd go to the gym three days in a row, look in the mirror for any discernible differences, have myself a good cry, and feel compelled to seek consolation at McDonald's on the way home.

Now I know that the primary benefits of healthful living—benefits that can be recognized almost immediately—are *energy* and *confidence.*

When I am disciplined in my lifestyle (regardless of what my bathroom scale has to say), I am a more confident person in my personal relationships, business dealings, parenting, and yes, even my lovemaking.

What health-related habits foster energy and confidence for you? My husband's cousin once told me she had not eaten any added sugar for an entire year. Was she trying to change her weight? No. Lori is an attractive, petite woman whose weight is not an issue. She had simply discovered that eliminating added sugar from her diet made her feel better. Find out what works for you, and make a conscious effort to incorporate these healthful habits into your daily living.

4. Put Your Best Foot Forward

You may have noticed that up until now my "recipe" for an improved body image didn't focus on making changes to our bodies. Instead, we've talked about adjusting our mindsets, examining values, and practicing healthwise habits.

What we've been doing, basically, is working from the inside out. Now, finally, it's time to tinker with what's on the surface: those elements that contribute to physical beauty.

Whenever possible, put your best foot forward. In makeup, hair, dress, and fingernails, even a small added effort can reap great rewards. It's amazing, for example, what a good haircut can do for the ol' self-esteem. And

Your body is the dwelling place of the Holy Spirit.

red toenails, even hidden beneath thick socks and a pair of boots, can make almost any woman feel sexier.

Buy silky lingerie. Buckle down and lose five pounds. Experiment with a new hairstyle or color. Wear bright earrings. Have your nails done. Get contact lenses.

Call your local department store cosmetics counter and arrange an appointment for a makeover. Most stores offer them free of charge. I recently made an appointment with a cosmetics consultant at Penney's. I happened to like the makeup she used, spent seventy dollars, and walked out feeling like a million bucks.

If there's something you can improve about the way you look, why not do it?

5. Pray

A lot of women begin working at the "skin deep" level which I've just described, and spend innumerable hours and countless dollars trying to assuage painful insecurities that lie buried far below the surface. The end result is frustration.

Physical improvements are most effective when coupled with diligent attention to inner dynamics such as the ones mentioned earlier in this chapter. Perspective, priorities, and the consistent practice of healthful habits *must* be considered in any campaign to improve the way you think and feel about your body.

And let's not forget prayer.

If you are embattled with insecurities about your body, take it to the Lord in prayer:

- Ask him to give you wisdom as you seek to unravel and discard your negative feelings and begin to develop a more positive perspective of yourself.
- Ask him to help you ultimately derive your self-esteem from your relationship with him, rather than from the image that is reflected in the bathroom mirror.
- Thank him daily for the body he crafted for you while you were yet in your mother's womb, for your health, for the balance of your days here on earth, and, finally, for the opportunity to serve him with a glad heart.

Remember, if you are a believer in Jesus Christ, your body is the dwelling place of the Holy Spirit. That in itself bestows an unfathomable value and worth to your physical frame, as flawed as you might perceive it to be. The great paradox is that if you are a believer in Christ, your body is the least important thing about you. One day your body will return to the dust and your spirit will soar to the heavens to live forever in the very presence of God.

As you wrestle with any insecurities about your appearance, these concepts might help you gain a balanced perspective. Ultimately, your worth as a human being is not derived from the color of your hair or the size of your nose; it is derived from your relationship with Jesus Christ. Your body is a tremendous gift that is meant to be cherished and taken care of, but in the end, its significance pales in the light of the health and well-being of your soul.

Maybe the previous paragraph doesn't really apply to you. Perhaps you've not yet asked Jesus Christ to become Lord in your life, accepting the gift of his death and resurrection as the single and best way for you to be reunited with a God who loves you. If this describes you, there may be no better day to remedy the situation than today.

Pray and ask Jesus to forgive the things you've done in the past that have distanced you from God; tell him you accept his death and resurrection as the means by which the distance between you and God can finally be bridged.

Ask him to send his Holy Spirit to live within you, making you sensitive to his ongoing direction and guidance in your life.

Ask him to help you connect with a Bible-based church and with other believers who can help you learn more about God and his plans for you.

Thank him for bringing you to this important crossroads in your life, for loving you enough to make it possible for you to be reunited with God, and for the transforming work he will continue to do in your life from this day forward.

If you've prayed this prayer, let someone know. Call a pastor in your city. Contact a friend or family member who believes what the Bible has to say and has been encouraging you to get right with God. You can even write to me; I would love to hear from you and support you in your decision.

Practice Fidelity and Commitment in Marriage

Stop me if you've already heard this one.

A man and his beautiful young wife were shipwrecked on a deserted island. They were not completely alone, however, for stranded with them was a handsome young sailor from their ship.

Every day this young sailor climbed the tallest palm tree on the island to scan the seas for signs of rescue. Each time he returned to camp, he chided the husband for not being more discreet: "You probably didn't realize it, but I can see everything from the top of that palm, and I saw you making mad, passionate love to your wife!"

Each time the husband denied the claim, the young sailor shook his head in amazement. "It must have been the sun in my eyes, but from up there I could have sworn I saw two people making love on the beach."

This same conversation took place several days in a row, until one day the husband decided to check out this phenomenon for himself. Being a little out of shape,

Too many of us just can't imagine "it" ever happening to us.

it took him a while to scale the rough trunk, but once amid the palms, the husband marveled at the view. "You're right!" he hollered down from his perch. "From here it *does* look like two people making love on the beach!"

It's easy to smile at a joke, even when it pokes fun at something as serious as infidelity. How nice it would be if infidelity were nothing more than fodder for comedians and authors of fiction.

Unfortunately, adultery is a real problem that too often strikes close to home and straight for the heart.

I have to admit that I was clueless as to the caliber of pain that infidelity can cause, until I was awakened in the middle of the night by the phone ringing by my bed. Upon discovering that her husband had a lover, one of my best friends phoned me at 3:00 A.M. screaming and weeping. She was alternately lucid and hysterical, livid and broken, as she vented the pain of a marriage betrayed.

It's difficult to count the cost of shattered trust. Even though we smile at stereotypes of cuckolded husbands and live in a society that continues to paint glowing pictures of the joys of unbridled sex, though we watch movies in which we are expected to cheer the budding romance of the heroine despite the fact that she's married to another, the truth is that adultery reaps a bitter harvest in every life that it touches.

Dispelling the Myth of Immunity

Despite the undeniably tragic ramifications of infidelity in homes all around us, too many of us just can't imagine "it" ever happening to us.

How many times have we listened to the latest gossip about the infidelity of some stranger or acquaintance, all the while feeling warmly smug in the myth that *our* marriages are somehow immune to that kind of temptation?

How many of us have inwardly smiled at the admirable—but inconvenient—precautions taken by other couples to keep temptation at bay? When I first learned that a friend of ours had a personal policy of never driving in a car alone with a woman other than his wife, I thought about all the times in my life I have driven in a car with male friends or colleagues. Was Billy going overboard with his policy? A lawyer, he certainly had just cause to spend time with clients, regardless of their gender. Was he taking "affair prevention" a little too seriously? Was I not taking it seriously enough?

For some reason, too many couples live under the misperception that adultery is something that happens to other people, and that their own marriages are somehow immune. When passions flare unexpectedly, they seem surprised, and yet people in-the-know—including pastors, counselors, and experienced married folk—are often clear in their warnings: Be careful and be diligent, for no marriage is beyond the temptation of illicit relationships.

I like to think of it like this: The question that should be asked by EVERY husband and wife, regardless of the strength of his or her marriage, is not: "What would I do *if* I were ever attracted to someone other than my spouse?" Instead, the question that every married man or woman should be asking is this: "How am I going to handle it *when* I'm attracted to someone other than my spouse?" Indeed, temptation is not merely a possibility. It is, in fact, more than a probability. If the truth were known, sexual temptation at some point and time in your marriage is virtually guaranteed. It is—along with death, taxes, and phone calls from vinyl siding salespersons during the dinner hour—one of the few guarantees you'll ever get in life.

In light of this fact, how can we stay faithful? How can we encourage our husbands to stay faithful? How can we manage our hearts and our desires, our thoughts and our libidos, in a manner that will protect our marriages and keep us pure before God?

Are You Faithful by Design . . . or by Default?

It's no accident that, in the title of this chapter, fidelity and commitment are paired with a very active verb: practice. Contrary to popular belief, fidelity and commitment are not practiced by the passive act of not doing something. In other words, the mere absence of an affair does not necessarily mean that you and your husband are practicing fidelity and commitment; it may mean simply that, so far, you have been lucky.

I have a friend who, I believe, may be an affair waiting to happen. This woman—I'll call her "Beth"—has not, to my knowledge, been unfaithful to her husband. Yet Beth appears to be taking few, if any, precautions to protect her marriage against the insidious destructions of an affair. While I don't want to make rash assumptions or stereotype a friend, I think I can safely assert that Beth's flirtatious manner—especially in light of her husband's frequent travels—is a liability to her marriage. In fact, sometimes her fidelity seems little more than a happy coincidence in the face of her panderings to other men.

I don't consider myself a big flirt, but as I'm sitting here writing these thoughts, I have to wonder: Am I so very different from Beth? I may not cater to other men or dress provocatively or stand a little too close to my husband's colleagues at the company Christmas party, but how "intentional" is my fidelity? Is it merely a happy coincidence, or is it strategically planned and practiced? Am I being faithful by design—or merely by default?

Fidelity and commitment in marriage are too foundational to be left to chance. Especially in light of the barrage of stresses, distractions, temptations, and all-out attacks being leveled at families today, it's imperative that husbands and wives take proactive steps to ensure the protection of their marriages.

Strategies for a Strong Marriage

Remember the friend I mentioned at the beginning of this chapter? Thrust into an unwanted divorce by her husband's continuing affair, my friend is, to say the least, a little wary of men. It is a stage of her grief which I trust she will be able to work through, but at the moment she sees an adulterer behind every bush. She eyes even the most stalwart husbands with suspicion, their wives with pity. Basically, influenced by the tragic demise of her own marriage, she is given (temporarily, I hope) to the philosophy that all men are scumbags and dogs.

It was while in this state of mind that Cathy shared with me her concerns about remarriage. She's not sure she can trust another man to stay faithful; she wonders, in fact, if any marriage can be safeguarded against affairs—and if it cannot, why subject herself again to such pain? Wouldn't it be better to stay single?

While there are no guarantees, I believe marriages can be safeguarded, and that there are strategies and techniques we can arm ourselves with today—before temptation strikes—that will protect our marriages against dangerous liaisons. Here are eleven suggestions for couples determined to affair-proof their marriages:

1. Accept That You're Not Immune, and Neither Is Your Husband

Author and psychologist Norm Wright, while being interviewed for another book project, told me: "People sit in my office and say, 'I never thought it would happen to me.' And before they tell me their story, quite often I can list for them, 'It started with this, and this, and this. . . .' There is no perfect safeguard for any marriage, but when a person says, 'Everything's fine at home,' or 'I don't need to worry about it. I'm safe,' those are danger signals. You always have to be on guard."

At about the same time, working on the same project, I interviewed Sylvia Nash, then director of the Christian Management Association. She had this to add: "Gordon MacDonald, well-known author and speaker, was asked some years ago, 'If Satan were to attack you somewhere, where would that be?' Gordon answered, 'Well, I'll tell you one area he wouldn't get me, and that's in my marriage. I have the healthiest and most wonderful marriage, and my wife, Gail, and I are deliriously happy.' One year later he had an affair, in the very area he claimed safeguarded. He and Gail have since rebuilt their marriage. The experience has left its scars but has also brought new depth to their ministry. We all think, *It could never happen to me.* And then all of a sudden Satan says, 'Oh yeah?' Satan is alive and well, so we'd better wake up. We *are* vulnerable."

2. Don't Neglect Sexual Relations

Whether sexual intimacy is neglected as the result of something as simple as an overbooked schedule or a more complex problem such as unresolved conflict in the marriage, the resulting void places both spouses at risk. By making a commitment to keep your love life consistent, intimate, and exciting, you and your husband will be nurturing one of the bonds that can keep you connected and focused on each other, even in the face of the myriad distractions and temptations the world has to offer.

3. Seek Professional Help for Unresolved Hurts No Matter How Small They Seem

It would be nice to think that all hurts between a husband and wife could be resolved by conversation, negotiation, time, and prayer. Sometimes, however, even the most dedicated couple can hit an impasse or a pocket of hurt that just won't seem to go away. Don't let something fester and take the chance that infected emotions will undermine your entire marriage. If you have been unsuccessful at resolving a conflict through other means, don't hesitate to seek pastoral or Christian psychological counseling. Getting help quickly can be the key to keeping molehills from turning into Mt. Everest and creating a barrier that will leave you and your husband isolated from each other and vulnerable to temptation.

Larry and I have personally experienced the "molehill to mountain" syndrome. At one point in our marriage we found ourselves fighting a losing battle with treacherous hidden currents in our relationship. I was clinically depressed; he was frustrated; we were both alienated and afraid and at odds with each other. Tackling the problem through Christian counseling was like three archaeologists digging backward through layers of muck and grime; we began with recent events and worked our way toward

Unresolved conflicts can be the prologue to a tragic tale of adultery and divorce.

the ancient. For a long time we worked with symptoms of our original problems, side effects that had taken on lives of their own and become problems in their own right: depression, anger, unforgiveness, denial. These problems had to be diffused before we could begin to dig deeper into new emotional territory. And you know what? As we did, I began to think to myself, "Wow, this isn't new territory at all; these issues look familiar." And they were. At the tail end of our experience with counseling, Larry and I found ourselves reunited with conflicts and hurts we had been unable to solve in our early years of marriage. Issues harbored, unresolved, had ambushed us years later in hidden forms.

I thank God that the temporary alienation Larry and I experienced from each other never resulted in adultery. But for many couples, the story of unresolved conflicts run amok is the prologue to a tragic tale of adultery and divorce. Don't let your marriage join the ranks of these.

Be diligent about keeping a clean slate and dealing with conflicts in a timely manner.

4. Practice Accountability

Norm Wright, in the same interview mentioned earlier in this chapter, admitted that accountability with his wife is one of the resources he uses to safeguard his own marriage. He told me, "If I am approached romantically by a woman, I talk about the incident with my wife, Joyce, for two reasons: one, as a safeguard, and two, so she's fully aware. Many times [extramarital] involvement has an edge of excitement about it because there is a forbidden aspect. When something is brought out into the open, a lot of the excitement evaporates." If you find yourself attracting romantic attention from someone other than your husband, confide in your husband or a trusted friend. And if you find yourself attracted to someone other than your spouse, my suggestion is similar: Tell someone trustworthy who will give you godly counsel and hold you accountable to remain pure in thought and deed.

5. Douse Temptations before They Flare into Sin

The Bible gives us two very prominent examples of how godly men dealt successfully with temptation. One example can be found in the fourth chapter of Luke where Jesus (who was not only a godly man but also our manly God) used his knowledge of the Word of God to put a stop to Satan's temptations. There are many Bible verses dealing with sexual purity, the hallowedness of the marriage bed, the importance of having godly thoughts, and so forth. Memorize a small arsenal of verses with which to combat temptation.

A second example in the Bible of a successful response to temptation can be found in Genesis 39:7–11. In these paragraphs, we discover how a righteous man named Joseph responded to an amorous come-hither glance from his boss's wife: He literally turned tail and ran from the room. There's nothing dishonorable or wimpy about someone who, when faced with temptation, simply runs. If you are in a tempting situation, remove yourself ASAP. Get out of the car. Leave the room. Hang up the phone. Change churches. Quit your job. Find new friends. Woe to the man or woman who expects that he or she can play with fire and not walk away blistered and scarred. Don't give temptations a chance to flame. Douse them immediately before they become too hot to handle.

6. Guard Your Thoughts

Contrary to belief, adultery doesn't begin with your lipstick on his collar and a hotel matchbook in your purse. Adultery begins in your thoughts and moves on from there.

A woman once confided to me that her affair began when she allowed herself the seemingly small indulgence of dwelling on her attraction to another man. George was a client wanting to buy a home through the real estate office where Susan worked as an agent. Each week as they toured the city looking for the home of his dreams she was dreaming too—about him.

In the beginning Susan believed she would be satisfied with her secret thought life. Whenever she felt a twinge of guilt, she assured herself she wasn't *doing* anything wrong; she was merely enjoying the rush she felt whenever she and George were together.

Before long, however, she began to suspect that he was attracted to her as well, and her thought life began to expand. Soon she was fantasizing about how nice it would be if they could verbalize their feelings about each other. She didn't want an affair; she just wanted to hear that he was as attracted to her as she was to him.

One day intimate joking did indeed lead to confessions about mutual attraction, and immediately Susan's thoughts rushed ahead to their first kiss. She daydreamed constantly about what it would be like to be held by George, despite the fact that she had her own family—a husband and two teenagers—at home. Several weeks later, they kissed for the first time, and Susan began at once to fantasize about making love.

As Susan's thoughts opened each forbidden door, her actions were not far behind in crossing the threshold. Just as the caliber of Susan's thoughts determined the caliber of her choices, your thoughts and mine are just as potent. Don't let unguarded fantasies trace dangerous paths for your actions to follow. For husbands and wives alike, protecting your thought life is a prime defense against the ravages of an affair. Pornography, romance novels, many R-rated movies, sexual fantasies about other people—even tabloid talk shows—can encourage our minds to cross thresholds that will weaken our resolve in the face of temptation.

7. Watch for Warning Signs

A few years back I cowrote a book entitled *Working Women, Workable Lives: Creative Solutions for Managing Home and Career* (Harold Shaw Publishers, 1993). In this book my coauthor, Linda Holland, and I included a chapter on affair prevention and recovery (which is, by the way, the source of my quotes from Norm Wright and Sylvia Nash). In this chapter Linda and I provided a list of warning signs for men and women who might not be willing to admit they are flirting with an affair. I've adapted the following list of warning signs from that book. As you

Don't let unguarded fantasies trace dangerous paths for your actions to follow.

can see, there are many boundaries that may be crossed mentally, spiritually, and emotionally before any action takes place that can be called "an affair." Both husbands and wives would be wise to recognize within themselves these internal red flags of warning:

- Do you find yourself making special trips past the desk of a coworker, or going out of your way to put yourself in the path of someone interesting at church or among your circle of friends?
- Have you taken new interest in what you wear or how you look?
- Is there a friend or coworker who makes you feel sixteen again?
- We all experience immoral thoughts from time to time, most of them fleeting. But are your thoughts drawn repeatedly to someone other than your spouse?
- Do you find yourself looking forward to meetings or events where a certain person will be in attendance? Long before you admit that you are attracted to someone, you may find yourself attracted to the places you'll be likely to see him.
- In conversations with family, friends, or your spouse, how do you talk about the person to whom you're attracted? Do you find yourself "forgetting" to mention seemingly innocent interactions? Or do

you find yourself drawn by opportunities to talk about that person or about the meeting or event at which you last saw him? Either approach is a bright red flag.

- When you think about that person, do you find yourself mentally justifying the relationship with phrases like, "We're just friends . . ."? Do you justify the relationship to yourself or to others with facts that are unrelated to the real issue? Linda and I interviewed one woman whose sister was the first to suspect trouble, asking: "Is there something going on between you and John?" The woman protested, "Are you serious? He's married with four kids." The sister was wise enough to respond, "That's not what I asked." The fact that someone is married or has kids or is a pastor or is the husband of your best friend has no bearing on how he may impact your heart.
- Has your prayer life gone cold? Are you as eager to read the Word and spend time with God in church?
- Do you dread intimate conversations with godly friends who might suspect something and seek to hold you accountable?
- What about music? Do sexy lyrics or melancholy love songs hold a new fascination? Do they pose a backdrop for new feelings of sensuality or thoughts of someone other than your spouse?

8. Respect Wise Boundaries

A woman recently told me she had been married for two weeks when her husband announced that he would be having lunch with a female colleague. This woman was surprised—especially since she knew her husband had once tried to date the colleague in question—but saw this as an opportunity to, with her husband, reestablish the friendship in a new light. She told her husband she would take time off work so she could join them. He shook his head saying, "You don't even know this person. She would feel awkward if you came. This is my friendship. I'm going by myself."

Was my friend's husband having an affair? Probably not. Was he practicing wise boundaries? Definitely not. Was he leaving himself vulnerable to sexual temptation? Absolutely. This marriage did, indeed, eventually crumble under the influence of an adulterous relationship.

Use wisdom in making choices and pursuing outside friendships. The "letter of the law" may say there's nothing wrong with going to lunch with an attractive coworker or making a business trip with a colleague of the opposite gender or getting together with an old flame. Yet don't allow yourself to fall into the trap of justifying your actions with the excuse that, technically, you're not doing anything wrong. Let wisdom and caution be your guides.

9. Practice Communication without Accusations

You've followed all the rules and then some. You and your husband have worked hard to keep your marriage strong and temptation at bay. Things are going smoothly, and you are confident your marriage is as safe as it can be from dangerous liaisons. Then one day you see, hear, or sense something that triggers a red flag, and you strongly suspect that one of your husband's relationships is not as neutral as it should be. You're confident your husband is not having an affair; he may, however, be flirting with temptation. What do you do?

In the course of life, there are times when relationships cross an invisible line and take on a hue of something more than friendship. It might happen to you; it might happen to your husband. Chances are, you both will have this experience many times in your marriage. We're all human, after all, and chemistry can spark between a man and a woman like spontaneous combustion, without prior planning or thought. It is not a sin to be attracted to someone other than your spouse; however, the litmus test comes with how that attraction is handled.

Get in the habit of talking openly and calmly about these matters—perhaps even before temptation occurs. Then you and your husband will be better prepared to approach a potentially explosive situation without adding fuel to the fire.

I know a pastor's wife who faced these precise circumstances. There was little doubt in her mind that a mutual friend was attracted to her husband. She didn't worry, however, until she began to suspect that her husband was enjoying the chemistry and, indeed, was attracted in return. While it might have been easy for this wife to confront her husband, claws bared and accusations sharpened, she chose a different tack. She shared her concerns quietly and rationally, all the while affirming her commitment to her husband and acknowledging his commitment to her and to their marriage. When he became defensive, she assured him she wasn't angry and that he hadn't done anything wrong—yet—which was the very reason she needed to address the subject. When he wondered aloud if she were jealous, she told him she was not. She said she was, in fact, confident in their marriage and in his love for her; rather than airing jealousies, she was instead making a calm observation and alerting her husband to a potentially dangerous situation.

In the end they both agreed that potential existed for trouble and made a commitment to handle the problem together, as a team. The outcome might have been different, however, if this wife had alienated her husband from the beginning with an irrational approach and unfounded accusations.

10. Extricate Yourself from Questionable Relationships

I could summarize all I need to say about this principle in six little words:

When in doubt, drop the friendship.

At first glance, it might seem harsh. It is, however, far less painful than confessing to your spouse that, yes, you've been involved with someone else, or having to sell the family home, or spending your first Christmas without your kids because you only get them every other year.

I hate to say this, but stronger marriages than yours and mine have fallen prey to the deceits of adultery. And while I don't want to scare, I do want to warn. When in doubt, get out. Regardless of the nature of the relationship—whether it is with a coworker, acquaintance, in-law, or friend—find a way to limit or eliminate contact altogether. Our first responsibilities are to our marriages; better to err on their behalf than flirt with the demolition of our very homes.

11. Pursue Spiritual and Moral Development

It's not uncommon in any given January to find people making lists of resolutions that include commitments related to career advancement, health, financial planning, or time management. It seems we're always looking to improve ourselves in every area, yet what kinds of commitments do we make when it comes to our spiritual and moral development? Just as neglecting sexual relations in marriage can create a void that leaves husbands and wives more vulnerable to temptation, a void in the area of spiritual or moral development can increase vulnerability as well.

How can we pursue development in these areas? Here are some ideas:

- maintain frequent communication with God through a committed prayer time
- stay in contact with godly friends who can encourage you through their words and example
- renew your heart and mind by reading and studying the Bible
- stretch your threshold of integrity through involvement with small groups and accountability partnerships
- and finally, add to your wisdom reservoir by attending retreats, conferences, and workshops related to topics like marriage, integrity, or spiritual growth

The tough news is that practicing fidelity and commitment requires a vigilant investment of attention. The good news is that the rewards are incalculable in their worth. Protecting your marriage begins today, before temptation ever strikes.

Newsflash . . . She's Here!

It finally happened. Six weeks ago, after nearly nine months of waiting, I gave birth to a beautiful baby girl. Kacie Jane joined our family weighing six pounds and ten ounces, sporting a fashionable mass of white-blonde hair, and screaming like a banshee.

She has a tiny pointed kitten tongue and porcelain-doll blue eyes. She makes the funniest O-shape with her mouth, a perfect circle, like she's blowing through a bubble wand, or perhaps is merely a little surprised at life. I'm enchanted, or can't you tell? What a miracle. What magic!

Labor was easier this time. Larry and I were calmer too. Eight years ago, when Kaitlyn was about to be born, we drove to the hospital at 2:00 A.M., pulled into an inexplicably full parking lot and drove around for five minutes before finding a vacant spot in the farthest corner. We had parked the car and were trekking across the asphalt—me in my bathrobe, leaking amniotic fluid, straddling a bath towel between my legs—when Larry said, "Gee, I guess I could have dropped you off at the door. . . ."

This time he got me to the hospital sans the quarter-mile hike. Oh yes. And when we walked into our LDR room, the first thing he did was turn on the TV to check out the reception. Yes, we were calmer.

What else can I say about the experience? Thank God for drugs, competent nurses, and speedy deliveries. How speedy? Larry waited until university offices opened at 8:00 to call in with the news that he wouldn't be coming to work that day. When he started the conversation, I was having contractions.

During the phone call, the nurse upgraded my status and told me to start pushing. As Larry hurried off the phone, I heard him say to his secretary, "I have to go now. . . . Karen's pushing the baby out RIGHT NOW!" Twenty-four minutes later Kacie was born. (Good thing my husband wasn't on the phone right then. I'd probably have heard him describing my placenta to the registrar.)

Anyway, the reason for this "newsflash" . . .

I had planned on mentioning Kacie's birth, casually, in the upcoming chapter, but somehow that didn't feel quite right. It would have been like calling a dear friend on the phone to talk about the upcoming Sunday school picnic and, halfway through the conversation, dropping the fact that you went into labor the night before and delivered your baby. I guess it seems like friends deserve to be let in on the great moments of your life with a little more intention and planning rather than as a mere "by the way . . ."

That's how I think of us, you know—as friends. We may never meet face-to-face, but I've thought of you daily as I've penned the pages of this book. That's why, I guess, I wanted to tell you the news not as author to reader but as woman to woman, replete with all the little details you'd hear if I had phoned you just to share the news.

So there you have it. Just think of these pages as a personal letter, or a quick phone call, or a birth announcement (which would, by the way, put you one up on a significant number of my relatives—most of their announcements are still sitting on an end table in my den, next to last year's Christmas cards).

Now, friend, on with the book . . .

Quarantine Stress and Distractions

You know there's too much stress in your life when . . .

- you find yourself looking forward to your next dental appointment as an opportunity to sit down and relax.
- you're in the habit of making midnight runs to the supermarket for either Rolaids or double chocolate fudge ripple ice cream.
- you've been trying since last April to read a book on how to reduce stress but can't get past the first chapter because the nervous tic in your left eye stresses you out when you read.

While it's true that some stress is necessary and even desirable, in the course of day-to-day living too many of us are living with an overdose. This is bad news for our physical well-being, since stress encourages headaches and heartburn and a wide spectrum of other maladies. It's also bad news for the well-being of our marriages; stress and distractions, after all, are two of the greatest enemies of romance and sexual intimacy.

Stress has been linked to impotency, an inability to climax, weight loss or gain, and depression. Stress can cause conflict between spouses, reducing the emotional intimacy that fosters good sex. Stress can rob us of sexual desire and impact our ability to enjoy the experience even if we agree to participate.

The good news is that stress and distractions can be managed. With some careful attention, it's possible to reduce the negative influence that stress can have on the quality and frequency of lovemaking.

How can we protect our love lives from the stress and distractions that make up a good part of our waking hours? Let's start by taking a big-picture look at the stress levels in our lives. For many of us, there may well be some general actions we can take to reduce our overall stress.

Big-Picture Stress

In trying to reduce your overall stress level, consider the following five tactics.

The first approach is to *unclutter your commitments.* If there's never enough time in your day, perhaps you should reacquaint yourself with the simple word *no.* Find a graceful way to eliminate some of the demands on your time. Once you have pruned your schedule back to a pace that feels comfortable, practice the *N*-word frequently.

Do not add anything to your schedule unless you can identify something else that can be dropped.

A second approach is to *simplify your environment.* If I could be honest with myself about this, I'd have to admit that half the stuff in every closet in my home is a promising recruit for the Salvation Army. If I had access to your

Aim for Southern Living in your private quarters even if the rest of your house looks like Mechanics Weekly.

closets too, we'd probably have enough to wage a small war. Declutter and simplify your surroundings, and you'll find more than closet space; you'll discover more emotional space and thinking space as well.

Third, *streamline your systems*. Is there an easier way to do something? I dreaded sorting laundry until I stuck three laundry baskets in our bedroom closet—a white basket for whites, a blue basket for darks, a green basket for sheets and towels. My laundry stays sorted, and it's easy to see when I have a full load.

Fourth, *tie up loose ends.* There's nothing more stressful for me than knowing I have five or six unpleasant tasks hanging over my head like anvils suspended by embroidery floss. Designate a Saturday (or a week or a month, depending on the number of anvils you're dodging) and wipe the slate clean. Write that letter; clean that closet; finish that overdue project; find the receipt the IRS has been pestering you about; mail that check.

Finally, *pick up the pace.* I wish I were talking about picante sauce, but it's not that simple. What I'm referring to here is, of course, the *E*-word. Exercise is one of the all-time great stress-busters. Unfortunately, our sedentary lifestyles seem designed to keep us from flexing three-quarters of the major muscle groups. Our ancestors, however, didn't lead such sweat-free existences; many of them sweated on a daily basis doing hard manual labor on farms. I am of the school of thought that says this daily exercise managed not only to eliminate stress, but also any negative impact stress might have had on the quality or frequency of sex (which is undoubtedly the reason old-time farm families frequently had ten or more children).

Create a No-Stress Zone for Two

After you've done what you can to reduce stress in general, turn your attentions for a moment to the place you and your husband most frequently make love. If you are like most couples, the place that comes to mind is the bedroom. (Author's note: The following suggestions are fairly universal. If you immediately thought of the laundry room, hall closet, or garage, these concepts can still be applied with only minor adjustments, so please read on.)

Turning your bedroom into a no-stress zone is simple. The idea is to intentionally design a relaxing environment that is off-limits to many of the stresses and

Sex, like exercise, is a clinically proven remedy for reducing stress.

distractions that define your waking hours. Begin with aesthetics, making an effort to keep your bedroom neat and attractive. In other words, aim for *Southern Living* in your private quarters even if the rest of your house looks like *Mechanics Weekly.* Then begin to work on behaviors, keeping your bedroom off-limits to activities other than sleeping, relaxing, or making love. Nix the stacks of unpaid bills, piles of dirty laundry, collections of unread newspapers, and file folders from the office. By fostering this kind of space, seemingly untouched by the nitty gritty of daily life, you will have created a quiet haven where—by simply stepping inside and closing the door behind you—you can take a mini-vacation from stress. This time can then be used to pray, to relax, or to lavish your undivided romantic attentions on your husband.

Enjoy the Benefits of Good Loving . . . before the First Kiss

Even if you follow all the suggestions in the previous paragraphs, there will still be times when it's 10:00 P.M., you should be making mad passionate love with your husband, and you just can't seem to empty your head of tomorrow's problems. They are, in fact, spinning around in your head about as quietly as a hamster on a rusty treadwheel. What do you do?

a. Talk your husband into forgetting sex and, instead, watching *I Love Lucy* reruns with you on cable.
b. Sneak down to the kitchen and spend a couple hours reorganizing your pantry.
c. Buy yourself a Habitrail.

There is another alternative. When you haven't been able to keep stress and distractions from joining you in the bedroom, try this little trick. Relax, breathe slowly and deeply, and imagine yourself half an hour from now, reaping the emotional and physiological benefits of good loving. Remember how it is? Basking in the aftermath of lovemaking, you feel different. Sensuous. Earthy even. Chances are, you're more relaxed, languid, content. As you stretch your limbs against the sheets, then curl against your husband with a little smile on your face, it's likely that tomorrow's problems won't seem nearly so troublesome.

By imagining the benefits of good loving ahead of time, we can help our minds and even our bodies begin to make a transition away from stress and toward romance. And in the end, our choice will have been the right one since sex, like exercise, is a clinically proven remedy for reducing stress.

So what are you waiting for? If a root canal sounds like R & R, if your need for antacids is exceeded only by your cravings for chocolate, if the nervous tic in your left eye prompts unfamiliar men to wink back and ask you for your phone number, there's no doubt about it. It's time for some stress-busting.

Reconnect Daily

It was December in California, and Larry, Kaitlyn, and I had flown in from Texas to visit our families for the holidays. The days between our arrival and Christmas Eve brimmed with a flurry of last-minute activities. Shopping, baking, wrapping gifts, more shopping, visiting relatives, visiting ATM machines for extra cash, decorating, vacuuming pine needles off the carpet, and discouraging my parents' dog Buddy from urinating on the Christmas tree were just a few of our daily holiday endeavors.

One evening we all hustled into the car to drive to a Christmas party at the home of family friends. We were a little behind schedule because my mom, sister, and I had gotten home late after spending a long day writing checks, signing charge slips, and bringing hysterical grins of joy to the faces of local merchants at a nearby mall.

Then again, perhaps I should say "maul" since we had been joined by 8.2 million other consumer types and had been lucky to escape the mad crush of holiday shoppers with our lives.

An hour later, my dad was behind the wheel, aiming the car loosely toward the freeway in a speed-limit-busting attempt to make up time. Makeup was on my mind too as I sat in the backseat and tried to whip on some mascara without losing an eye. Kaitlyn, in turn, had her eye peeled for any police cars in the vicinity because she knows that's what I do whenever I'm driving and my own speedometer needle crosses into the red zone.

In the midst of all this holiday fun and frivolity, my mom looked across the front seat at my dad and said, "Whew! What a busy day! I feel like I haven't seen you in a week!"

My dad grunted, checked the rearview mirror, and changed lanes at something approximating the speed of light.

My mom, oblivious to the fact that we were about to blast into hyperspace, reached over and twirled a lock of my dad's hair around her finger. "I know! Let's look at each other. For just a minute. In the eyes."

My dad responded this time. He groaned. "Honey, I'm driving!"

"Ten seconds. Five! I haven't seen you all day. I need to look into your eyes. Are you ready?"

He shook his head. "I can't look right now, Geri. We'll have a wreck!"

"At the next light."

At the speed we were traveling, we hit the next red light in no time. And sure enough, holding hands across the front seat, my parents turned and gazed into each other's eyes. "Hi," my mom said. "Hi," my dad said warmly back.

Then the light changed, the gas pedal hit the floor, the engine roared, and the race was on again. Kaitlyn still listened for sirens and I still flirted with blindness. Nothing had changed, and yet everything had changed. Most of all, I was silently moved by what I had witnessed: a small harbor of reconnection in a raging hurricane of activity and distraction.

Life in the Fast Lane

It's not easy to stay connected with our husbands, is it?

My husband recently received a promotion at work, becoming provost and chief academic officer at Dallas Baptist University. We're both excited about the new challenges, and yet longer hours associated with the transition have taken a toll on time spent at home.

How much of a toll?

Recently Kaitlyn was telling her dad about what she termed "the bestest dream I've ever had in my life." In describing the dream, Kaitlyn began to name the characters who had peopled her sleep. She named me, her friend Laura, Laura's mom, Rachel and her mom, Kaitlyn's first grade teacher Mrs. Parks, Mrs. Parks's two daughters, and last but not least, a life-sized animated Ken doll who escorted Kaitlyn and her friends to the toy department in J. C. Penney's to pick out *any* toys they wanted free of charge. (Really.)

About that time Larry said, "What about me? Wasn't I in the bestest dream you've ever had?"

Kaitlyn considered this question a moment and then said, "No, you were at work."

Ouch.

We've all felt his absence. A couple of weeks ago my friend Cherie landed a job at the university where Larry works. When she told me the news, she added, "And don't worry—I'll keep an eye on Larry and report back to you every day. After all, I'll see him more than you do!"

Luckily, this pace should be temporary. Then we will experience an estimated three to five days of "normalcy"

Many women say that lovemaking without emotional connection leaves them feeling "used."

until the next promotion or book project or illness or holiday season or any of the other daily life events that serve to pull and pummel and stretch and test the bonds between husband and wife.

But then again, Larry and I hardly have a corner on the market of fast-paced living, do we? My guess is that you, too, know what it's like to feel that the pace of life is raging out of control. Like it or not, if you are like me, there are simply times when marriage seems more about logistics than love . . . when your most intimate conversation in a week contains the words "dry cleaners" . . . when your relationship with your husband is best characterized by two ships passing in the night—with both helmsmen asleep from exhaustion at the wheel.

Reconnecting with Our Husbands in Body and Soul

So what does all this have to do with sex?

Nothing.

And everything.

It's true that sex—even great sex—can take place in the absence of emotional intimacy. But at its very best, sex is the union of two bodies, two hearts, two souls. Someone once observed that "when sex is divided from love there is a feeling that one has been stopped at the vestibule of the castle of pleasure." I believe the same can be said of the experience of two people who love each other, but who have lost that emotional connection in the pell-mell pace of daily living.

In fact, many women say that lovemaking without emotional connection leaves them feeling "used." Perhaps more than our husbands, we need to make the effort—daily!—to reconnect with the men in our lives, and to somehow communicate to them how emotional reconnection can energize our love lives and our marriages too.

But how do we go about it?

The Teeter-Totter Principle

Emotional reconnection is not unlike a teeter-totter—when you're up for it, you can be fairly certain that your husband won't be, and vice versa.

In fact, statistically speaking, there is a fairly high chance that if you are feeling the need to reconnect, your husband will be thinking about reseeding the front lawn. By the same token, when your husband is pondering the possibility that you and he have drifted emotionally, chances are you will be in the midst of planning a sit-down dinner for thirty-seven.

What are the odds of this happening?

Statistically speaking, they are about the same as the odds of the phone ringing as soon as you step into the shower, or the odds that one of your kids will get chicken pox on the day you have a major presentation at work, or the odds that on the evening you run to the store for a can of coffee twenty minutes before your husband's boss and his wife are due to arrive at your home for dinner, you will find yourself in the only checkout line with a trainee cashier.

In other words, it's virtually guaranteed.

When this happens, it's easy to make a single overture of reconnection and then fling up your hands in despair and surrender. My mom, after all, could have given up at the first "Honey, I'm driving!" But she didn't. She persevered. And, eventually, her message hit home.

Someone once said, "Consider the postage stamp. Its usefulness consists in sticking to one thing till it gets there." When you feel the need to reconnect and he doesn't, don't give up. Stick with it. Rephrase, reframe, and repeat your message, and eventually it will get to where it needs to go.

The Day-Timer Principle

Believe it or not, you and your husband *can* be in sync about reconnection. On the same day, at the same time, you can each make an equal commitment to the task of reestablishing the emotional bond that will enhance your marriage and your love life.

As we've already seen, you cannot rely on "feelings" to drive this kind of synchronized commitment, because the chances are great that this won't happen by coincidence.

It can, however, happen by calendar.

Carol and Stanley have been married for nine years. Even before their marriage, during the time they were dating, they set a precedent that has survived the test of time. Every Wednesday of every week of every month of every year for nearly a decade, they have planned a date. Together. Alone.

That's 468 dates. And counting.

Carol says that they don't always spend a lot of time. Or a lot of money. Sometimes their "date" consists of sharing a plate of nachos and a couple of Dr. Peppers at a local Mexican restaurant. Other times they get up early, before the kids arise, to share a quiet breakfast together. Sometimes they meet for lunch. Occasionally they go to see a movie.

The only requirement is that each Wednesday they carve out a niche of time in which to be alone, to talk, to reconnect, without kids or friends or phones.

Carol says, "I have a lot of women friends who say to me, 'My husband and I never have time to just sit down and talk.' I have no doubt that Stanley and I would be in the same boat if we didn't make the effort to set aside this time, just for us. It doesn't have to be major—it just has to be a priority."

The Pavlov Principle

From deep in the archives of our high school education, most of us are familiar with the story of the Russian scientist who performed experiments in behavior modification by training canines to salivate at the sound of a bell.

While I am not suggesting that you train your husband to do the same (although it might be an interesting icebreaker at parties), there is something to be said for conditioning.

If dogs can hear a bell and think of food, why not come up with a word or a ritual that will remind your husband—and you too!—of special, connected times you have shared? Indeed, the frequent use of a familiar word or ritual may very well be the transition that can quickly move you and your husband from separate places of isolation into the shared terrain of reconnection.

It might be as simple as, in the case of my parents, developing the habit of reconnecting via very conscious

Sometimes a touch can synchronize emotions in ways that mere words cannot.

and intentional eye contact. It might be a special pet name that you use during your most intimate and connected moments; calling your husband by that name at other times will remind him of tender moments you have shared. Perhaps a ritual such as a back rub can serve as a familiar transition.

We tend to think of "ruts" as negative. But that's not always the case. It's true that through repeated patterns of behavior you can carve into your marriage a hurtful and dangerous furrow that is easy to fall into and difficult from which to escape. The good news is that you can also practice patterns of tender words and deeds that can rapidly become, as you retrace them over the years of your relationship, furrows and then gullies and then canyons that bring incomparable depth and beauty into your marriage.

The Epidermis Principle

There is one last principle on which you can rely when trying to get off the roller coaster of life and reestablish emotional contact with your husband. It's called the Epidermis Principle.

That's right, skin.

Bodily contact.

Close encounters of the physical kind.

Never underestimate the power of touch as a means of triggering emotional reconnection. A touch, hug, kiss, or massage can synchronize emotions in ways that mere words cannot.

Even the act of lovemaking itself can provide a profound sense of emotional reconnection. "A tender sex life brings out our best qualities," says marriage therapist Roger Falge. And why not? The best sex is, after all, an intense integration of vulnerability, communication and trust, sensation and pleasure and touch, expressed in the most intimate dance of give-and-take.

Sex is, and always has been, irrevocably and irretrievably linked to the greater depths and hidden springs of who we are as individuals. In the words of J. L. Casserley, "Human sexuality is too noble and beautiful a thing, too profound a form of experience, to turn into a mere technique of physical relief." Our sexuality shapes, and is shaped by, our very psyches and must be viewed in the context of the whole. A satisfying sexual bond between a man and a woman simply cannot stand alone, apart from our sense of emotional integration. The quality of each drives the other.

Developing a strong emotional bond with your lifetime mate should be easy.

Unfortunately, it's not.

It can be done, however, and done well, with a little planning, effort, and attention on your part.

Safeguard the Lover Within

Four months ago I really suffered.

My husband insisted that I fly with him to Maui.

Now stop rolling your eyes and let me explain why I initially perceived this as somewhat of an imposition. At the time of our trip I was seven months pregnant. Unlike Demi Moore, I didn't think of myself as prime cover girl material. Bathing suits and waxed bikini lines were not words currently peppering my vocabulary. Hit the beach? If I hit the beach, I'd cause a tidal wave.

In other words, I was not feeling my most glamorous or amorous self at the moment. When it came to the thing most prominent on my mind, necking was out and nesting was in. There were, after all, rooms to paint and baby clothes to wash and meals to cook ahead and stash in the freezer. And I had these precious little twenty-minute increments between bathroom breaks to accomplish all these great feats of domesticity. Basically, I was feeling pretty maternal, which is why, as I found myself skimming my things-to-do list, flying to Maui didn't exactly emerge as a burning priority.

Let's face it. There are times in a woman's life when the label on the hat she's wearing says anything but "lover." There are other things on our minds, other roles we are being required to play. And in the grand drama of family life, there can be moments, perhaps even months or years, in which it seems far more enticing to spend our energies perfecting our roles as mothers and hope that our husbands don't complain too much about our lackluster performances during the love scenes.

This was, for me, a temporary mode. It's not unexpected, while expecting and even while raising young children, to feel a rush of maternal feelings that can eclipse other emotions. And yet I have always admired women who, while excelling at motherhood, manage to keep a portion of their lives reserved for themselves and for their spouses. Yes, they are mothers. But they are also individuals and women, and when it comes to their husbands, they are friends and even lovers.

Mother, Lover . . . or Both?

Lover. What a wonderful word. It's something most of us want to have and want to be. Yet this is easier said than done.

In the midst of all the hustle and bustle of our busy lives, romance can seem like a luxury, especially for women with small children at home. Too often the role of being a mother seems to be in conflict with the role of being a romantic lover. After all, the title of mother seems to encompass so many different hats and responsibilities—from chauffeur and chef to maid and mentor—that there just doesn't seem to be any time or energy left to reprise, with our husbands, the roles that started it all—the roles of man and woman, our roles as lovers.

Listen to what these mothers had to say about the role of romance in their lives:

"My husband and I used to do all these spontaneous, fun things together. Romantic, sexy things. Then we had kids and all that fell by the wayside. To live the way we lived before seems impossible now."

"I feel guilty spending grown-up time with my husband. Shouldn't I be spending that time with my kids?"

"I wish I had more energy for sex, but after a full day of give, give, give to everyone else, it just doesn't seem like a big priority."

The fact is that even if we work very hard to carve secluded moments in which to set aside our "mommy" hats and concentrate entirely on our relationships with our husbands . . . well, it's not uncommon to experience a twinge or more of guilt at the prospect. It's not unusual to feel, you know, a little selfish at the thought. Which raises the following questions:

- Is it selfish?
- Does time spent nurturing our sexuality detract from our roles as mothers?
- Shouldn't the needs of our young families preempt our needs as individuals and women?
- Or do we have a responsibility—to ourselves, our husbands, and even to our children—to keep our sex lives alive and vibrant?

The Conflict Resolved

I believe there is no conflict of interest between motherhood and loverhood. In fact, the bond that is created by sexual intimacy between you and your husband does far more than enhance your relationship alone—it also enriches the lives of your children. That's right! The best mothers are not those women who devote every waking moment to their children. The best mothers are, indeed, those women who take the time—make the time—to cultivate, protect, and express the lover within. Here's why:

A happy love life is one of the best defenses against affairs and possibly even divorce. If you ever fall into the trap of thinking that making time for marital romance might detract in some way from the lives of your children, stop a moment and think about how much more they would be affected if either you or your husband had an affair or filed for divorce. Frequent sex does not, of

How do women manage, in the midst of pabulum and purple dinosaurs, to still think of themselves as lovers?

course, guarantee a happy home. And yet a loving and intimate physical and emotional bond between husband and wife is undeniably a welcome harbor in the frequently turbulent seas of marriage.

A happy love life establishes harmony in the home. One woman I interviewed explained it like this: "When sex loses priority and falls to the bottom of the list, there's a brokenness in my relationship with Mike. We're not connected. We're each in our own little cubicles, seeing the world through tunnel vision, pursuing our own agendas. When this happens, I see the ramifications throughout the family. Even my kids react. They're out of sync as well. They're grumpier, don't do their chores, don't follow through.

"About that time, Mike will start to send little signals to me that seem to say, 'You don't have time for me,' and

Moms and dads are people too, with needs of their own.

I know it's true. I realize I'm acting like I don't have time for him. I have to rethink my focus: Am I more committed to my schedule than to my husband?"

Darla went on to add: "With two busy schedules, we have to work a bit to keep sex a priority. But once we do, it usually filters down through the ranks. When our relationship is cohesive, when we have communication between us, when the quiet, unspoken stuff between us is in harmony, everything's better in the household. For everyone."

A happy love life creates a healthy model for our children to follow as they become adults. Why do we so often assume that our children don't know what's going on in our homes? They do, you know. They see and hear far more than we think they do. And even if they don't fully understand what they are seeing and hearing, the words and images stay with them and help shape their perspectives as adults.

I remember, for example, seeing subtle signs of sexuality between my parents. Sitting at the kitchen table watching my mom fix him a sandwich, my dad would suddenly pull her into his lap for a kiss. At other times, when she thought we kids weren't looking, my mom would flash my dad a subtle wink. Many were the Sunday afternoons my sisters and I would knock on the locked door of my parents' bedroom and whine, "You've been in there for an hour! We're bored! When are you coming out?" to which my mom always replied languidly, "We're resting. Go play and we'll be out soon."

Now that I'm a wife and mother, it doesn't take a lot of brainpower to figure out the reasons behind those long Sunday siestas. But at the time, I was clueless. All I knew was that my folks seemed to have some secret between them . . . a pleasant secret that made them happy. Those images, even without being fully understood at the time they were recorded, went a long way toward helping me develop a positive perspective of sex and sexuality as something wonderful to be cherished and enjoyed by husbands and wives.

Safeguard the Lover Within

How do women do it? How do they preserve their perspective as romantic, sexual beings? How do they manage—in the midst of pabulum and purple dinosaurs—to still think of themselves as individuals, women, and even lovers?

Some women find that a little self-pampering—a bubble bath, manicure, or new piece of costume jewelry—helps rekindle memories, attitudes, and perspectives from their "pre-children" years.

Spending grown-up time with your husband is another key. You may remember, from earlier chapters, Carol and Stanley, who reserve each Wednesday for their weekly "date," or Diane and Doug, who manage to escape together for a long weekend three or four times each year. These are good examples of couples who have made long-term commitments to spending grown-up time with each other. Alternatives might be as simple as reconnecting via a gaze at an intersection, or making a deal with your husband to turn off the TV one night a week just to talk.

Finally, help your children to understand that you and your husband need grown-up time together. Model healthy boundaries for your children. Moms and dads are people too. They have needs of their own, and sometimes this includes a need for private time. Your commitment to "grown-up time" will not only enrich your marriage and strengthen your home; it will also prepare your children to make the same healthy choice in their own marriages.

Kids often think that they are the very center of life and that the universe somehow spins just for them. And you know what? They're almost right. It's easy, as mothers, to allow our lives to revolve around the children with whom we have been blessed. And yet it is for the good of our marriages, ourselves, and our children that we sometimes allow ourselves to be pulled out of their orbit. Remember who you are inside, beyond the roles and titles and responsibilities you have assumed. Covet and create opportunities to express your sexual self and seek the fulfillment of your needs, and every member of your household will benefit.

Transition from Routine to Romance

If your life is anything like mine, the word *routine* is a bit of a misnomer. *Routine* implies some sort of habitual occurrence, a system even. Unfortunately, the only thing habitual or systematic at my house is chaos.

Last night, for example, I got up with Kacie seven—that's SEVEN—times. I fell asleep twice today sitting in a chair and once leaning on the kitchen counter, prompting Kaitlyn to pontificate about the accuracy of the old wives' tale that horses are the only creatures that sleep standing up. I drove to the dry cleaners and to Kaitlyn's jazz class and to the gas station and to the grocery store where I spent thirty-one dollars on cold medicine and bought sixty pounds of sugar. (What can I say? They were running a good sale.) I activated the smoke alarm once while cooking dinner, spent several hours ordering my eight-year-old to get ready for bed "THIS INSTANT," and now it's 11:00 P.M. and I'm praying for a quiet hour in which to write before Larry gets tired of providing comic relief for a teething baby.

Perhaps *routine* is a bit ambitious. A better word to describe my day-to-day life might be *anarchy.*

And when it comes to romance . . . well, there are few words that are more hilariously out of place in the life of a new parent than the word *romance,* although occasionally I think I remember what romance is. If I'm not mistaken, it's the thing that made me a mother in the first place.

The problem, then, seems to boil down to this: How to get from A to B, A being utter chaos and B being sex. This might be possible except for the fact that the sex part has some unrealistic requirements, one being the absence of any children and another being my ability to stay awake for more than three minutes after lying down.

I'm sorry. Here I am, complaining like I'm the only one whose life doesn't resemble a Jane Seymour perfume ad. Chances are, you've got your own troubles, your own reasons why at times it may be difficult to make a transition from point A to point B, from chaos to ecstasy.

So what do we do about it? Sit back and let our love lives go the way of the saber-toothed tiger and the wooly mammoth? Hardly. With a small investment of effort, it's possible for us to improve our skills at creating effective transitions between routine and romance.

Transitions Take Time . . . So Clock in Early

Too often by the time the kids are in bed, the dishes are done, and you've scanned the office reports you were supposed to have read last week, your energy level is subterranean. When your husband starts doing his hubba-hubba walk toward the bed at 10:15, you don't need a transition; you need a pair of jumper cables.

What's a woman to do? One solution is to nix the element of surprise. Responding to a surprise requires much more energy than responding to something you've been thinking about half the day. Tomorrow night, don't wait until you're running on empty and then try, in ten seconds or less, to go from zero to sixty on the vavoom meter. Start earlier in the day to warm your engine so that, by 10:15, you just need to be nudged (rather than towed) toward Lover's Lane.

Some couples, for example, make a "date" with each other in the morning for fun and games that night. Knowing that late-night romance is on the agenda helps some women pace their energy throughout the day.

I agree that it can be helpful to make a verbal commitment in the morning to make love that night—now let's take the concept one step further. During the day, DO one thing in anticipation of the pending romantic interlude with your husband. On your lunchbreak, pick up a bouquet of flowers to sweeten your bedroom. When you get home from work, take a quick shower and slip on something feminine under your clothes for your husband to discover later. Knowing that a heavy meal can make you feel sleepy and sluggish, plan a light supper instead. Spritz your bedsheets with perfume. Spend five minutes straightening up so that your bedroom looks a little more like something from the pages of *Good Housekeeping* and a little less like your neighbor's driveway the last time he had a garage sale.

Making a small effort that will contribute to romance with your husband will go a long way toward preparing you—mentally, emotionally, and physically—for the encounter.

Ask for Customized Transitions—And Don't Forget to Return the Favor

Okay, pretend once again that it's 10:15 and time for the hubba-hubba walk. If this transition leaves you feeling listless, the problem may be, as I've discussed in the previous paragraphs, the late hour and the fact that your energy is already depleted.

It's also possible, however, that part of the problem may be your husband's choice of transition. In a perfect world, our husbands would always know the precise combination of words and deeds that would render us ready for romance. In real life, some "transitions" work better than others.

For example, research statistics indicate that in nine out of ten American bedrooms, the phrase "Hey, honey, wanna get lucky?" is decidedly less effective than, say, a back rub and the offer to make the kids' sack lunches for the rest of the week.

I know one woman who says that for years her husband's transition of choice has been to approach her while she's in the middle of some project and ask, "Do you want to make love?" She loves making love to her husband but would prefer a different transition. After all, if she had been thinking about sex, she would have been seducing her husband rather than feeling perfectly content watching the weather channel and folding socks. She knows that given about ten minutes in which to switch gears she will want very much to make love, but having to make the transition in time to give the right answer to her husband's pop quiz is always a challenge.

I believe in the interest of good marital communication it is okay to talk openly about the transitions that work best for us. Your husband, like that of my friend, may need some new ideas about more effective methods of lighting your romantic fires. Likewise, it's a good idea to ask our husbands for some clues as to the transitions that work best for them.

A few days ago I took my own advice to heart. I asked Larry to describe three methods by which he would like for me to approach him when I'm feeling amorous. Likewise, I gave him three "scenarios" describing ways in which I would like to be approached romantically. We then made a commitment to put into practice what we learned. I have one month in which to use the three transitions that Larry described for me; he, in turn, has one month to use the three transitions I outlined for him.

Consider making a similar request of your husband. By customizing your transitions to fit individual tastes and whims, you and your husband can maximize your effectiveness at building bridges between routine and romance.

Take a Familiar Shortcut

Married love has taken a beating from some secular philosophies. These philosophies imply that monogamous matrimony is mundane while swinging singlehood, complete with a variety of sexual partners, has more to offer.

Yet while these philosophies take potshots at the routine of married sex, I believe it is precisely that routine which can impart some of lovemaking's nicest moments. In other words, routine can enrich, rather than detract from, the sexual experience.

When you love someone for many years, the routines of preferred positions, favored environments, familiar quirks, and even predictable come-ons enrich your love life in many ways. For starters, they create lasting memories. I also like to think that they provide small harbors of familiarity and comfort in a world that too often seems spinning out of control with hostility and change. These familiar routines can also create reliable transitions—tried and true triggers—to help you cross the bridge into romance. These triggers can, in effect, serve as shortcuts that can take you quickly out of your separate worlds of work and friends and car pools and deadlines, and into your intimate, shared world of lovemaking.

Let me give you an example. One woman I know admitted that for the beginning years of her marriage she and her husband rarely made love without first setting the mood with romantic music. Their artist of choice was David Sanborne on the saxophone. To this day, this friend can't listen to saxophone music without becoming aroused. In fact, one day while driving home from work she made the mistake of listening to sax music on the radio and ended up getting a speeding ticket while trying to get home quickly to her husband.

Other examples: Several friends of mine consistently use bedroom candles to create a romantic atmosphere before sex. Another friend shared that, for years, Sunday afternoons have provided a reliable, quiet haven for lovemaking. One woman I know admits that humor provides a familiar and welcome transition into sexuality: As soon as her husband approaches her and says, in a mock-serious voice, "Julie, there's something I'd like to get straight between us," she knows how the encounter is going to end.

Just as there will be times when you'll appreciate an early announcement and lots of time to make the transition from your role as mother/employee/household manager into your role of wife/lover, there will also be times when a quick, familiar, reliable transition will do just fine. During your marriage, be on the lookout for pleasurable routines that help you and your husband transition into lovemaking. Make an effort to repeat these routines often. They will become even more effective with practice.

Understand and Accept Your Differences

A couple weeks ago Kaitlyn and I snuggled onto the den couch with a bowl of popcorn to watch a rented movie video. Before our main feature began, however, we were subjected to previews for other films. One of these was a movie entitled *He Said, She Said* about differing perspectives between the sexes. When Kaitlyn didn't understand some of the nuances of one of the scenes, she turned to me for clarification.

"They're fighting because men and women have different perspectives about life. You know, because they think differently," I explained.

"Men and women think the same," Kaitlyn announced authoritatively.

"Not really," I said absently, watching the screen.

"I don't think they think differently. How do they think different?" she persisted.

"You'll notice it more when you're older," I said, aware that our feature presentation was beginning.

By now Kaitlyn was growing impatient. "I don't want to wait. Just tell me real quick. Ten words or less. What's the MAIN difference?"

Explain the differences between the sexes? In ten words or less? How about ten thousand? People have

Our differences go beyond whether we leave the toilet seat up or down.

been writing about gender differences since the discovery of charred wood, and we still don't have it figured out.

Despite androgynous fashions and gender-inclusive terminology and politically correct philosophies about the sameness of men and women, differences abound, and more often than not they get the better of us.

I mean here we are, going through life innocently trying to have marriages with the men that we've married, and we keep getting tripped up by the irritating fact that, well, they're not us. They're not even *like* us. Despite the fact that husband and wife are supposed to be one in the eyes of God, that we're supposed to be soul mates and forever friends and lovers for life, we are reminded daily that our spouses are members of some foreign club with rules, jargon, secret signals, and rituals all its own.

Take, for instance, the way football players are always patting each other's tight ends—and on national TV no less. What exactly is that all about? When plays are slow and commentators are digging into pigskin archives to come up with something to analyze, why don't they ever explain that patting thing?

And what about selective hearing? Why is it that a man who swears he never heard you say you wanted him to go with you to the PTA meeting can listen to a car engine and hear a pin-drop "ping" that even Sprint would have a hard time picking up?

And let's not even get started in the bedroom. Why do men and women have such different views on what it takes to get ready to make love? Why is it that most women prefer taking the slow train toward arousal while many husbands opt for the space shuttle? And how can they walk out of the bathroom ready to make love, while we emerge merely ready to get ready? Don't they know that brushing and flossing do not count as foreplay?

Yes, sometimes our men are difficult to understand—and of course they say the same about us. And in the end, it's far too easy to allow our differences to drive subtle wedges between us.

A far better alternative is to learn how to understand, accept, and (bear with me on this one) even grow to cherish the little differences that are scattered like stumbling stones throughout even the smoothest marital path. Of course this may seem easier said than done, but let's consider some insights and suggestions that just might help us reduce the battle between the sexes to a few drills now and then rather than a civil war.

Understand That Men and Women Are Not Cut from the Same Cloth

Some differences can be linked to the fact that your husband is, well . . . a man. Despite current politically correct thinking, men and women *are* different, and the differences go beyond whether we leave the toilet seat up or down.

By learning about some of the documented differences between men and women when it comes to sex, work, relationships, and even our thinking processes, it just might help you cope with behavior that until now may have been driving you nuts. Let's begin with a quick look at some lovemaking mismatches:

For instance, knowing that men are really on a shorter fuse for arousal—that they are created that way and are not just being impatient—may help you be more understanding as you negotiate mutually satisfactory transitions in the bedroom.

Understanding that men are wired in such a way that they are aroused primarily by *sight* just might encourage you to let your husband win the lights on/lights off battle now and then.

Knowing that it takes a woman's body (heart rate/body temperature/blood flow) about fifteen minutes to return to normal following intercourse—while a man's body snaps back virtually immediately—might help you avoid feeling resentful when he starts rattling the bedposts with his snores just as you're cuddling close for an intimate postcoital snuggle.

And physiological behavior in the bedroom isn't the only thing that can be chalked up to gender. While there are exceptions to every rule, even the thinking processes of men and women appear to be divided into two camps. Perhaps you've already heard the analogy of men and women and their dressing room counterparts. The first time I heard it, it made a lot of sense, and I knew it was a pretty good way to look at one of the key differences between men and women.

Men, they say, are like dressers—a collection of separate drawers, if you will. As such, men operate one drawer at a time, focusing on the contents of that drawer to the exclusion of all others. Work, marriage, friends, kids—even sex—are somewhat compartmentalized and separate from each other.

In contrast, women are more like walk-in closets. With each item in our lives visible from virtually anywhere in the closet, we tend to view our lives as an integrated whole rather than as a series of compartments.

This is, of course, the reason a man can go merrily off to work and never cast a second thought to his three children at home with fevers and a babysitter. His wife, on the other hand, will think nothing of putting the company president on hold while she completes her sixth call home since lunch to check on her kids.

The fact that he functions best in "compartments" is also the reason a man will get frustrated when he's trying to talk to his wife and is interrupted for the third time by whiny children. His wife, however, can cook dinner, soothe a toddler's "owie," warn a third-grader away from the cookie jar, answer a homework question, and still catch every word of her husband's version of the argument he had that morning with the contractor who is remodeling the upstairs bathroom.

So how does this relate to the bedroom? When a man opens the compartment of his life labeled "sex," he may well be able to concentrate wholly on the moment, temporarily shelving everything else in his life. It may not be so simple for his wife. If she feels distracted by other details of her life, she might not feel particularly amorous. If her husband only has to open a drawer to get in touch with his sexual side, she may well have to mentally reorganize her whole life in order just to find hers.

This is why a man can focus on love despite a hectic day at the office. His wife, on the other hand, may well be trying to climax while mentally composing the family Christmas letter that has to go in the mail by Wednesday.

Likewise, a man can get in a big fight with his wife, and two hours later at bedtime be ready for romance. Unfortunately for him, about that time his wife is probably still wondering how, next time she does laundry, she can short sheet just one side of the bed.

Understanding that men and women come to the table with basic, ingrained differences can help ease the tension during moments when we might otherwise be tempted to take something personal and become angry or resentful.

Accept That Every Personality Has a Few Quirks

While some traits can be chalked up to gender, others are of a, well . . . individual nature.

While treadmilling at the gym recently, I found myself browsing through a copy of *Glamour* magazine. I found an article so funny that I ended up asking the girl at the front desk if I could take the magazine home with me. The article included excerpts from a book entitled *I Love Him But* . . . by Merry Bloch Jones, which quotes women on the most annoying habits of the men they love.

Like what, you ask? How about the woman in California who complains that her husband "can never remember our PIN number at the bank machine—which is annoying because it's our anniversary date."

Or how about the wife from Cleveland who says of her husband, "Every night, settling into bed, he grunts. He sighs a long sigh and groans the same, predictable words every single night: 'Oh, bed, bed, bed, bed, bed. Oh, bed, bed, bed, bed, bed. Oh, bed, bed, bed, bed, bed. Oh, bed, bed, bed, bed, bed. . . .'"

Then there is the woman who writes, "When [my husband] offers to help around the house, he asks so many questions and gets so confused that it's easier to do everything myself. If he were going to boil an egg, for example, he'd ask, 'Which pot should I use?' 'Does it matter which burner?' 'How hot do you set the burner?' 'How long should the water boil?' 'Do you put the egg in before or after the water boils?' 'Do you time it from when you put the egg in or from when the water boils?' 'How much water do you put in?' 'Which egg should I use?' 'Where are the eggs?' 'Where's the pot?' 'How long does it have to boil again?'"

As far as I can tell, these are not universal traits among men (thank goodness). But even though you might not see any of these behaviors at your home, that doesn't mean that your husband doesn't have his own equally amusing (or annoying) behaviors.

Sometimes the differences are not humorous at all, but can leave us feeling puzzled and hurt. One woman, for example, admitted that she was devastated when she discovered she had married Scrooge's twin brother. "For the first six years of our marriage, he wouldn't acknowledge Christmas," she remembers. "We often fought when I spent money on the kids for presents, and he absolutely

There's just some stuff that doesn't warrant drawing the proverbial line in the sand.

refused to go shopping and buy anything for me. Looking back, I began to realize that even dating he had never given me big gifts at Christmas. I took it personally. I didn't understand and I was hurt by his behavior."

For this woman, healing came as she learned more about her husband's past and grew to accept this part of his personality. "Eventually, I came to understand what had happened. His grandfather—who he had loved dearly—had died on Christmas Day, so that time of year continued to hold sad memories for him. Instead of staying mad or fighting to change him, I began to compensate. I continued buying gifts for our children and also began each year to buy a Christmas present for myself from my husband. At first he was surprised; then he seemed relieved. Now, after I spend the day shopping, I go home and tell him, 'You bought me my Christmas gift today,' and he smiles."

She adds, "Fighting is a wonderful thing. You can fight for three years or five years over something, and then finally you get it figured out. You gain a better understanding of what makes your man tick—and he understands you better, too—and you are able to accept each other. My husband knows now that every year I'm going to go shopping, put his name on packages—including a package for myself—come over to him in front of everyone and give him a big kiss, give him all the glory. And I understand, too. I can accept who he is and not feel hurt anymore."

Cherish the One You're With

Understanding and acceptance go a long way. But what if we took the whole thing one step further? Is it possible we might actually grow to *cherish* some of the characteristics that set our husbands apart from us? Now of course you and I both know that marriage requires a goodly amount of negotiation. There are some behaviors that husbands (and wives) bring to marriage that are hurtful or destructive and need to be addressed. I obviously am not talking here about conflicts of that magnitude. Besides, we all know that it pays to choose our battles. There simply is some stuff that does not warrant drawing the proverbial line in the sand. These, then, are the kinds of issues that we can understand, accept, and even grow to appreciate and cherish.

The fact is, often the small quirks that set our teeth on edge are "side effects" of more encompassing personality traits that we love. For example, I may become annoyed when Larry goes to get a glass out of the kitchen cupboard and informs me it would be more efficient if the glasses were on shelf two instead of three; yet I love the fact that he is a creative problem solver who always seems to know precisely how to handle the bigger crises in our lives. Is it possible to see the two behaviors as sides of the same coin? If so, my appreciation for his problem-solving nature in general just might help me be a little more gracious during those occasional moments when he tries to "fix" something that, in my book, isn't even broken.

What about your marriage? Is there a way to mentally "repackage" some of your husband's traits you like the least so they can be viewed in light of his finer qualities? Is it possible to remember that the same competitive drive that is so annoying during a friendly game of Uno is a godsend when your husband is selling his employer's products out in the field? Or that the same testosterone level that reduces him to a Neanderthal on Super Bowl Sunday makes him a tiger in your bedroom on Saturday night?

The minor irritations of marriage can cause big-time erosion when it comes to emotional and even physical intimacy between spouses. Don't let small bothers sabotage marital harmony. When it comes to even the best of relationships, a good dose of tolerance just can't be beat.

Vent Your Anger

The Bible gives good advice when it admonishes readers "not to let the sun set" on their anger, and yet that is often easier said than done. And to make matters worse, it seems there's no one who can get under your skin quite like a spouse. After all, more than anyone else, he knows all the right buttons to push during an argument!

I'll never forget one argument Larry and I had. Of course, I've already forgotten the cause of the fight; all I remember is the fury I felt at whatever marital breach of contract Larry had so callously committed. I was so furious, in fact, that it seemed to me the only reasonable response was for me to walk to his side of the bed, pick up his alarm clock, and throw it out of our second-story window.

Despite what you must be thinking right now, I am not typically prone to committing acts of hostility against helpless housewares. To say that afterward I felt foolish would be like calling the Washington Monument a pet rock. I apologized afterward, but it didn't quite seem like enough. I made plans to buy Larry a new alarm clock and present it to him with a note that said "I guess you don't have to be having fun to make time fly," but he repaired the old clock and forgave me my juvenile fit based on my verbal apology alone.

It's inevitable in any marriage for tempers to flare. In fact, it's more than inevitable—it's even healthy! The real issue is what we manage to do with our anger once it erupts. There are, after all, constructive ways to express and dissipate anger.

And then there is the alternative.

Mishandled anger is one of the archenemies of the successful marriage. My little tirade is one example. But perhaps even more harmful than a burst of misdirected fury is anger that isn't expressed at all. I call it gopher anger because, like a burrowing rodent among the roots of a prized garden, repressed anger causes the most damage when it isn't even seen. Oh, occasionally it rears its bucktoothed head and squints into your face, but most of the time it stays underground, destroying the very foundation of your marriage.

Vented correctly, anger is a normal dynamic of any intimate relationship. Unfortunately, when it is misdirected or repressed, anger undermines emotional intimacy, it can develop into bitterness, and it can even cause depression. And there's little question that it wreaks havoc with a love life! It's hard to be vulnerable, after all, with someone you'd be willing to trade in for a new kitchen appliance.

As you seek to develop a repertoire of healthier responses to anger, consider these suggestions:

Think about it. Anger by itself isn't necessarily dangerous or wrong. Even Jesus experienced anger when he confronted the money changers in the temple! In marriage, as in life, there are times when anger is a legitimate and healthy response to something going on around us. There are other moments, however, when anger isn't justified and may even be able to be dispelled with a little analysis.

Several months ago, for example, Larry spent a grueling week backpacking in the Grand Canyon with friends. When I picked him up at the airport, it was after midnight. He hadn't slept in two days or bathed in four. He was tired and triumphant, exhausted and exhilarated, as he told me some of his adventures during the drive home. About the time we pulled into the driveway, however, conversation turned to how things had gone at home during his absence, and upon learning how I had resolved some small matter while he was gone, well . . . Larry snapped. He huffed. He fumed. He criticized. If he was frustrated, I was livid. I was so angry with his overreaction that I marched in the house, truly determined to go on strike as homemaker/secretary/lover until I had been the object of some serious groveling.

Then I thought about it. For the past week this man had been sleeping on rocks, eating freeze-dried pellets, hauling a pack on his back the size of a small farm animal, and pushing his body to perform hiking feats under which most twenty-year-olds would have folded. Yes, he had snapped at me, but somehow I wasn't angry anymore. He did apologize the next morning, but that's hardly the point. Sometimes just trying to see things from your spouse's point of view can go a long way toward soothing small conflicts.

Talk about it. There are times, however, when a mere attitude adjustment just doesn't cut it. Sometimes you know you've got to try to clear the air. Try to select a time when emotions aren't running high. Then, when you talk to your husband, don't focus as much on what he did wrong as on how his actions made you feel. It's important when talking about your anger to make your primary

Living angry is no way to live.

goal the act of expressing yourself, with your husband's response to you merely a side issue. If you go into the conversation with the goal of obtaining a particular response—such as an apology—from your husband, you may be disappointed and come away even angrier than before.

Write about it. During an angry season in my own life, some of my greatest moments of insight, forgiveness, and recovery came from writing about my anger in a journal. Sometimes the person you are most angry with isn't nearby for you to talk to; or perhaps you've talked to him, but your words have fallen on deaf ears. Try writing letters to the person you are angry with, to God, even to yourself.

Sweat about it. A tense moment can cause your body to pump up your adrenaline level. And even when the moment is passed, you may still feel tightly wound as a result of the chemical changes the anger brought about in your body. Take a brisk walk around the block, weed your garden, vacuum your house, work out at the gym. You may well find that a spurt of physical activity will burn away the excess adrenaline and leave you feeling calmer and more clearheaded.

Pray about it. Sometimes anger and bitterness take root so deeply that prayer is among your best resources as you strive to wrestle free of anger's grip. The problem in this case may not be so much that you are angry, but that you are unwilling or unable to forgive. Remembering that our unforgiveness toward others can hinder God's forgiveness of our own sins, ask God for help in forgiving and letting go of past hurts.

Get counsel for it. There's much to be said for wise and godly counsel from a friend, pastor, lay counselor, or psychologist. Sometimes it helps to hear someone say, "I understand why you're angry; you have every right to be upset. Now how can I help you move on from here?"

The bottom line is that living angry is no way to live. Emotional and physical intimacy with your husband—the very stuff that marriage is made of—will simply not survive and thrive in an anger-ridden atmosphere. Occasional fights and disagreements and lovers' quarrels and bursts of tension are as much a part of the marriage game as making love and paying bills. The key is to make a clean sweep after each and every angry moment, finding healthy ways to vent your feelings and reconcile your relationship with the one you love.

Write Your Own Story

Kaitlyn has already nicknamed her. Dozens of times, in fact. Kacie Jane is a.k.a. The Kacer-Pacer, The Cutester, and, when she spits up or poops, That Gross Baby. Ah, the joys of sisterhood.

You know what gets me? The personality differences between the two girls. Same parents, same stock, but it's already evident that Kaitlyn and Kacie have entirely different outlooks on life.

Kaitlyn, for example, was intense even as a baby, and she's an intense child now. Kacie, on the other hand, may be a native Texan, but her demeanor is California Casual for sure.

Kaitlyn slept through the night at three months, Kacie at three weeks.

Kaitlyn's frequent cries could usually be comforted by the nipple, her daddy's special "flying baby" hold, or when all else failed, a midnight car ride on the freeway. Kacie gets upset once every three weeks—but when she does, batten down for a wild one, because there's no stopping her.

Luckily for me, I was never naive enough to think that raising Kacie would be a repeat performance of my experiences with Kaitlyn. If I had, I'd be scrambling to make some mental adjustments about now, because the girls are already as different as night and day.

Any parent with more than one child has a similar story. We all seem to know and understand that no two children—even with the same parents, even *twins*—are alike. On the contrary, each new life is like a fingerprint, a snowflake, a sunset like a million others and yet altogether unique and one-of-a-kind.

We know this about our children.

We don't seem willing to accept this concept when it comes to our marriages.

If we truly understood the one-of-a-kind nature of our marriages, we wouldn't be so inclined to compare ourselves to the marriages of friends, the relationships of

Can't we just learn to relax and enjoy what we have?

fictional characters on TV, in movies, or in books, and most importantly, the couples represented in the latest *Redbook* magazine survey on bedroom antics.

You know it's true. Some women's magazine runs a survey claiming 98 percent of married couples do it twelve times each week and we all experience a 41 percent decrease in the size of our sexual egos.

The idea that, somewhere, there exists a sexual standard for successful marriages, some secret volume of *Roberts Rules for Relationships*, a marital measuring stick, well, it's just plain silly.

Garrison Keillor wrote about the idea of a benchmark in this way: "Somewhere, when I was young, I got the idea that the average American couple had sex twice a week, and I've carried this figure in my head for more than 30 years. . . . Probably the [average] American couple has carried the old twice-a-week standard around in its head and in those weeks when there is only one sweaty encounter has felt that something must be wrong. Probably that feeling of not meeting one's sexual quota is what drives the multibillion-dollar diet industry and produces all those identical magazine articles about 'Ten Ways to Make Your Marriage Sensational.'" ("It's Good Old Monogamy That's Really Sexy," *Time,* 17 October 1994, 71.)

So why do we do it? Why do we compare? Why do we build our expectations for our own marriages on assumptions about the marriages of other people? Can't we just learn to relax and enjoy what we have, without continually peering around to compare ourselves to what we think others have?

In the intimate dance between husband and wife, there is no master bandleader, no two-step instructor, no choreographer. You and your husband have to figure out what works for you.

In the division of labor around the house, in child-rearing responsibilities, and especially in the bedroom, there are no experts other than the two of you. Throw out the surveys and work on negotiating a plan for romance that meets the approval of two people and two people alone: you and your husband.

Write Your Own Romance

Growing up, I was a sucker for fairy tales. Even as a young adult, I'd walk into a bookstore and make a beeline for the children's section, leaving the store more often than not with some oversized picture book, preferably something featuring princesses and castles, tucked under my arm. When I became engaged to be married, I broke the news to my family that I wanted to be married in a park, at dusk, and that as the ceremony drew to a close, Larry would mount a white horse, lift me into the saddle behind him, and ride with me into the sunset.

Much to Larry's relief, about that time one of my grandmothers intervened and said she wasn't keen on attending a horseback wedding in the park. I was a little perturbed at having to choose between her and the horse, but in the end, Larry and I were married in a traditional church ceremony.

One of the great things about fairy tales is that they follow a pattern, so you always know what you're in for when you crack open the book. Oh sure, there's room for a few twists of plot, but basically you know how the story is going to begin ("once upon a time"), how it's going to end ("happily ever after"). You know the hero and heroine are going to have to overcome challenges (three of them, in fact), and you know you're going to close the book wallowing in warm fuzzies.

Real life, as we know, is another matter.

The bad news is that our marriages are not products of the imagination of Hans Christian Andersen. The good news is that we have the profound joy and privilege of writing our own stories, unique, one-of-a-kind sagas where predictability has no place, where we are both heroine and author, and where every page tells a tale unlike any other.

Exalt Your Spouse

One Sunday morning a couple of weeks ago I made an announcement to a handful of couples in a Bible study class Larry and I attend. The announcement went something like this:

Help.

I told them I was at the tail end of my manuscript, and that it had finally happened: After eighteen months, twenty-three chapters, and more than two hundred pages I was finally running low on things to say. I told them the title of my current chapter was "Exalt Your Spouse" and that I would hang around after class to talk to anyone who had any thoughts to contribute to this chapter.

First I was approached by Jack, an articulate thinker who always has something insightful to contribute to group discussions. My pulse raced in gleeful anticipation of some gem of wisdom from this godly husband and father.

"You know, Karen," he said, "after hearing your request, I tried to think of something having to do with the word *exalt*, and nothing really came to mind. That's when I began thinking about other *X* words you might want to consider. I thought of *X-ray*. If you don't have any luck with exalt, maybe you could change the title of your chapter and do something with *X-ray*." Jack, by the way, is a neurologist.

As Jack moved on, I was approached by Bill and Linda, married for nearly three decades. Surely I was in store for something wonderful.

"When Linda and I first got married, we made a pact," Bill said.

So far, so good.

"The pact was that throughout our married life I would make all the major decisions and Linda could be in charge of all the minor decisions."

I wasn't sure how this was going to relate to exalting spouses, but I continued listening intently.

Then Bill grinned. "The interesting thing is that, in twenty-eight years of marriage, we've never had to make a major decision." Linda must have heard this one before because she was smiling even before her husband delivered the punchline. I knew I'd been bamboozled, but I had to laugh anyway.

That's when Rick stepped forward. He smiled sheepishly as he told me his thoughts, but his were no joke. "I tried to think about what I do to exalt Gayle, but all I kept coming up with was things I do that I shouldn't. I should be patient, but too often I'm impatient. I should praise her more, but it's so much easier to fall back on critical words. If you need some examples of what not to do, I'd be happy to be interviewed. Better yet, ask Gayle—she probably has a long list." Then he shrugged, "I wanted to try to help you out, but . . . oh well! Guess I wasn't much help at all!"

Yes, you were, Rick. And Jack and Bill and Linda too.

How? You provided me with the best possible illustration of a critical fact: Exalting our spouses, unlike breathing, blinking, or eating chocolate, does not come instinctively to the human race. Asked to come up with some thoughts about exalting their spouses, a class of twenty-some adults provided me with one joke, one confession, and the suggestion to go with an easier topic!

I don't blame them.

It's not easy to exalt the spouses whose faults, flaws, and foibles are on display every day. And yet the way we treat each other as husbands and wives—whether we cherish or chide, dignify or demean, humiliate or elevate—can shape our relationship, establish the atmosphere of our homes, and determine the level of intimacy we share in the bedroom.

To Exalt or Not to Exalt

What exactly does it mean to exalt our husbands? I'll admit that *exalt* isn't a word that peppers our everyday vocabulary, but the definition of this old-time term is simple enough. It means to enhance the status of someone or something.

In other words, exalt means to honor, to build up, to elevate, enhance, or uplift. The opposite is to belittle, detract, minimize, or degrade.

Which collection of words best describes the impact of your words and deeds on your husband and on your marriage? Do your words and deeds enhance his status in your eyes, in the eyes of your children and friends, even in his own perception of himself? Or do your words and deeds more often cut him down to size? Keep him humble? Deflate his ego? Keep him "in line"?

You may well be wondering what this has to do with emotional or sexual intimacy. Well, actually quite a lot. When we look for opportunities to exalt our husbands, the following dynamics are likely to occur.

- Our husbands may gain more confidence in themselves as worthwhile individuals, fathers and breadwinners, husbands and lovers.
- Our husbands may experience new, positive feelings toward us; we might even notice an increase in quality and/or quantity of time spent with our spouses. This isn't such a far stretch of the imagination, is it? You and I aren't so different. We all want to spend time with people with whom we feel appreciated and esteemed.
- You and I will probably experience new, positive feelings toward our husbands. After all, it's not easy to feel kindly toward someone we've been badmouthing all day. On the other hand, after spending the day focusing on the better qualities of the men we married, we may well find our hearts have warmed in response.
- When a husband and wife make a daily effort to exalt each other, great sex is often a natural result. After all, it doesn't take much of a transition to go from being loving to making love. One woman, married more than four decades, explained it this way: "Kindness leads to gentleness, which leads to tenderness, which leads to . . . you know." In other words, for the kinder, gentler couple, transitioning into romance can be virtually effortless.

Seven Ways to Exalt Your Lover

So how can we build up, esteem, elevate, and honor our husbands? Let's start with something simple.

1. Treat your husband at least as well as you treat your friends and colleagues. It might not sound like much, but the sad fact is that often our best behavior is reserved for chums, colleagues, and acquaintances, while our harshest tones and snippiest comments are doled liberally to the husbands and children we love the most. Take the experience of a woman I interviewed last week. Approaching her golden wedding anniversary, Billie has four children, twelve grandchildren, one great-grandchild, and a working knowledge of what it takes to exalt a spouse. When I asked her to comment on this subject, she told me about the time, several decades ago, when she and her husband invited a seminary student from their church to live with them for a year. She admitted that having a permanent houseguest encouraged her to dust off her company manners to use at home. She pondered, "Why do we have different codes of behavior for outsiders and for our own family? Having this young man live with us for a year taught me a lot about myself. I love the members of my family more than anyone else in the world. I realized I wanted to treat them that way all the time, not just in public or in front of company."

2. Let your tone do the talking. Don't tell me I'm the only one who has gotten into arguments over stuff I didn't even say! Last week, for example, I told Larry it was okay if he went to see a movie with one of his friends. Larry, being a sensitive and observant sort of guy, picked up on the fact that while my words said, "Go ahead and have fun," my stony tone managed to add: "and may you be infested with the fleas of a thousand camels for going off and having a good time and leaving me home alone when you KNOW I've been housebound for a week with the flu and a book deadline and two kids, one of whom is teething and another for whom the words *It's bedtime* comprise nothing less than a call to nuclear war, THANK-youveryMUCH."

For some reason, even when we manage to keep our words in check, our tones can take on lives of their own, communicating our frustration, anger, impatience, disappointment, or apathy in point-blank fashion. Let's face it. There are certain tones we feel free to use with our husbands that we would never think of using on a friend: Glacial tones, clamped-teeth tones, nuclear blast tones, even tones that manage to convey subtle messages like "Boy, did I marry a numbskull" or "If you think you're getting any tonight, think again, Sherlock."

Shame on us. Whether we realize it or not, uncivil tones are great esteem-busters. Rather than engaging in guerrilla warfare with hypocritical words booby-trapped with hidden poison, a better choice is to voice our concerns in a patient and loving manner. Words, after all, are open to discussion and analysis. They can be rephrased and renegotiated until both parties have come to a common understanding. Uncivil tones are not so easily tamed. Instead, they tend to slip by unchecked, inflicting small wounds in the very hearts and souls of those we love the most. A loving tone, on the other hand, is a balm that makes even unpleasant words much easier to bear.

The fact is, when someone wants to understand the true attitude of our hearts, the tone with which we speak usually reveals far more than the words that we say.

3. Body language says a lot. How can we use body language to esteem and elevate our husbands? Sometimes a little nonsexual touching conveys much. Billie admits that she and her husband end every mealtime prayer with an "Amen" and a kiss, even if they are dining out in a restaurant. For more than fifty years, my grandmother and grandfather held hands each night as they drifted off to sleep. My friend Diane says that the way to make her husband David feel loved—more than words or deeds—is touch, and that holding hands, a back rub, or a hug can always raise a smile.

Then, of course, there are times when body language isn't about physical contact. Have you ever noticed that the very best listeners listen with their whole bodies, not just with their ears? You know who I'm talking about—I'm talking about those people who make conversation a pleasure because they seem to be absorbing your every word with something akin to hunger. They lean toward you slightly as you speak, they engage you in eye contact, they nod their heads at appropriate intervals, and if you're really lucky, they practice what is perhaps the most desirable body language to be found in an effective listener—their lips are closed. Talking with someone who understands the art of listening is, without a doubt, a status-building experience. When it's all over, you feel validated and esteemed. You know that you've been heard and quite possibly understood. You may even feel grateful.

Now compare this to how you listen to your husband. If you're like me, there are too many moments when you may be listening with your ears, but the rest of your body is engaged in a variety of other pursuits ranging from opening a can of spaghetti sauce to rinsing out jars for the recycling bin to wiping a toddler after a bathroom break. While flushing the toilet, you suddenly notice your husband has stopped talking and you holler, "Go on, I'm listening," only to discover he's no longer in the house; he's in the garage changing the oil in the family van. The sad part is that he's been there for twenty minutes.

4. A little appreciation goes a long way. Do you make a habit of expressing appreciation to your husband for all that he does for you and for your family? Or do you spend far more time reminding him of all the things he's not doing? You and I both know how our esteem can plummet when we feel unappreciated in the face of all our efforts on behalf of our family. Our husbands are no less undermined by underappreciation, and no less buoyed when their daily efforts meet with rave reviews. In her book *Fascinating Womanhood* (Bantam, 1992), Helen Andelin suggests that women learn to express appreciation of positive traits in their husbands' character such as honesty, dependability, kindness, or love. We can also verbalize appreciation for our husbands' intelligence as it is expressed through education, knowledge, good judgment, or creative imagination. Finally, we can be appreciative of all the things our husbands do for us, from earning a living to opening a car door.

5. Admire manly features. In the same book mentioned above, Andelin tells women that while *appreciation* draws attention to a man's character and intelligence, *admiration* draws attention to his masculinity. That's right—to elevate your husband's esteem and enhance his status, admire his manly qualities. According to Andelin, these include his masculine body, skills, abilities, achievements, and dreams. She goes as far as to say that while the center of a woman's happiness in marriage is to be loved, the center of a man's is to be admired. So go ahead . . . tell your husband what broad shoulders he has . . . what strong muscles he has . . . what sharp teeth—whoops, sorry, wrong story. Seriously, make an effort to affirm and admire the masculine traits that set your husband apart as a man, and both you and your husband will benefit from the results.

6. It doesn't pay to be funny at your husband's expense. I've always been one to appreciate a good one-liner. I'm even more fond of funny anecdotes. And yet all humor is not created equal; it can take on a destructive, cutting edge that wounds more than entertains. Good-natured ribbing occurs in nearly every family; the key is to make sure that the jokes don't hit too close to home and cause hidden hurt or embarrassment.

7. *Perspective can make the man.* Finally, when you look at your husband, what do you see? The father of your children? The man you fought with last week and made love to last night? A breadwinner? Someone who hogs the remote control?

Sure, there are lots of little things you can do to exalt your husband. And yet "effective exaltation," so to speak, isn't rooted in the things you say and do as much as in your overall attitude. With the right attitude and perspective, you won't have to think about ways to make your husband feel esteemed; it will happen naturally.

One of the ways to adjust your attitude is to bring your perspective in line with the viewpoint of someone who knows your husband far better than you ever will. That's right—the God who created your husband knows that you are married to a creation of inestimable worth and value, ripe with potential, a melting pot of skills, gifts, and abilities.

Yes, yes, I know he does annoying things. My husband does too. Recently I came home after spending a week in California and discovered that Larry had childproofed the entire house. Then again, the word *childproof* may be a misnomer. I suspect that David Copperfield couldn't move freely around our home.

Nevertheless, I praised the plastic locks on the kitchen cabinets. I expressed appreciation for the new Velcro thingamajig that restricts access to our entertainment center. I tolerated the fact that I can no longer raise the toilet lid unless I return to college and obtain a degree in mechanical engineering. And I experienced homicidal urges when I discovered that the plastic protectors on the four corners of my prized four-hundred-dollar hand-painted coffee table had been mounted in a semi-permanent fashion using SCREWS.

In that moment, blinded by the sun glinting off the silver heads of eight behemoth screws embedded in the beveled edges of my table, what was my perspective of my husband? Let me just say that exalting him was not in the forefront of my mind. Execution, however, was an enticing possibility.

What was God's perspective? No doubt the Creator of my husband looked down and saw a protective father, an ingenious problem solver with a slight bent toward overkill, and a human soul well worth the unfathomable price of the life of God's Son, Jesus Christ, nearly two thousand years ago.

Do you want to exalt your husband? Ask God to imbue you with his perspective, a God's-eye view that is breathtaking in its scope, in which a vast and imperfect landscape glows like spun gold in the light of the Son, where small flaws and foibles are as easily overlooked as a crumpled Coke can on the side of a ribbon of road far, far below.

EXalt Your Way to EXcellent SeX

Yes, sex is for procreation. It is also designed to provide physical release. And sometimes, even in the most godly marriages, it's just for fun—a lusty romp in the sheets after the kids are finally asleep.

But more than anything else, the best loving is rooted in the small kindnesses, uplifting words, and gentle gestures exchanged daily by husband and wife. Treat your man like a prince throughout the day, and you just might be surprised at the royal treatment that awaits you both when the sun goes down!

Say Yes to Biblical Boundaries

I have a friend—I'll call her Penelope—who is a true Southern belle. She was born and raised in Georgia. She is vivacious and hospitable. And she's got this really great drawl.

While drinking cider and downing chili dogs at my daughter's school's fall festival recently, Penelope and I got to talking about men and women and marriage. She waited until our husbands wandered back to the concession stand for some nachos, and then she told me this story.

When she met and fell in love with her husband, Frank, they hailed from two different worlds. At twenty-five, Penelope had lived a protected life. She still lived at home. She was a virgin. She was wide-eyed with idealism and naiveté and anticipation. Frank, on the other hand, was a thirty-four-year-old Navy man who had just recently come to know the Lord. He had two children, an ex-wife, and a working knowledge of worldly living.

During their engagement, the couple received the standard premarital counseling session at the church they were attending. This included a personality test that Penelope and Frank were asked to take separately, reviewing their answers together later.

After the test, Penelope and Frank sat together in the pastor's office and compared their answers. They were thrilled to see that, more often than not, their answers complemented one another. That is, until they hit question number forty-seven. The question was: "Do you consider yourself sexually inhibited?"

Frank's answer was yes.

Penelope had answered no.

Flabbergasted, Frank turned to his Southern belle bride-to-be. "No? What do you mean you're not inhibited? What are we talking about here? Handcuffs? *Threesomes? Animals!?*"

Penelope nearly fainted. Catching her breath, she managed to blurt, "Well, darlin', no! I just meant I'd be willing to do it with the lights on!"

Are You Inhibited?

When it comes to sexual inhibitions and boundaries, the continuum seems vast, as Penelope and Frank discovered during their counseling session!

Candidly speaking, there are a lot of options out there when it comes to sexual expression, and the list seems to keep growing. According to King Solomon, there's nothing new under the sun. And yet it seems the media is always informing us of some new bedroom technique that most of us have never heard of before. You may remember one made famous (or infamous) by Princess Fergie: toe sucking. According to articles in women's magazines, this is supposed to be very sensual, although personally I wouldn't know. After spending fifteen years picking up a man's discarded socks, the idea of putting his toes in my mouth does not keep me awake at night with longing. But maybe that's just me.

Yes, we have options. Choices can range from leaving the lights on or turning them off to deciding whether or not to use the eggbeater this time around (just kidding!). So, where do we draw the line? Penelope drew her line at the light switch. What about you and me? Are we too inhibited? Are there secret techniques we're missing out on? New erotic experiences the neighbors know about and we don't? Are there things we should be willing to try with our husbands? Are there experiences we should avoid at all costs?

What *are* healthy sexual boundaries for married couples?

Inhibitions from the World's Point of View

According to some modern-day authors of books and magazine articles, there are no boundaries. One article I read recently suggested that faking orgasm can improve your marriage. The author went on to describe how to breathe and moan to make your performance more realistic.

Another author, in her current best-selling book on sex, writes about a woman who claims that having an affair with a coworker actually enhanced her marriage and love life with her husband of eleven years.

Finally, there are countless articles that assure women—and men as well—that it's a great idea to fantasize about other people while you are making love to your spouse.

Luckily for you and for me, if we have a living relationship with Jesus Christ, we don't have to take our cues from the world. We are protected from the ramifications of random, anything-goes experimentation. As we've already discussed, God is pro-sex. Any guidelines he sets down are not to diminish our sexual pleasure, but to protect and enhance it!

Inhibitions from a Biblical Perspective

So what does the Bible have to say about healthy sexual expression? First, let's look at things the Bible tells us specifically not to do. Basically, the Bible says no sex before marriage, or with anyone who is not your spouse, including relatives, prostitutes, animals, or someone of your same gender. These guidelines go on to include "mental sex," or dwelling on sexual fantasies about someone other than your spouse.

These are the specifics. In a way, they say a lot. Translated into "socially acceptable" behaviors and lifestyles of today, these guidelines prohibit living or sleeping together before marriage, homosexuality, prostitutes, swapping spouses, affairs, and pornography.

But in other ways, these guidelines leave a lot to the imagination. Sexuality between a husband and wife, in the context of marriage, can be expressed in any number of ways that are not mentioned at all by Scripture. Does that mean anything not specifically prohibited is okay?

I interviewed one women who said, "I have a lot of questions. There are some things I'd like to try with my husband, but I'm embarrassed to bring them up. I mean, should a nice Christian woman *want* to do the things I'm curious about?"

The Bible is silent on a number of "gray" areas such as masturbation, sex toys, oral sex, talking "dirty," sexual games such as role-playing, bondage, costumes; and I really do have to wonder what God would have to say about sucking toes!

Even though the Bible doesn't give us specifics, I think there are biblical principles that can shed some light on the subject as we make decisions about what's okay—and what's not okay—in the bedroom.

Temper Your Choices with Love

To begin with, Ephesians 5:25 tells us that *husbands should love their wives as Christ loves the church.* When I think of this verse, I think of the gentleness of Christ. He doesn't use force. He doesn't humiliate or manipulate. Love and self-sacrifice are hallmarks of his relationship with believers and with the church as a whole.

How might this attitude between a husband and wife impact bedroom politics? Forcing a spouse to have sex is out. So is forcing a spouse to engage in any type of activity that makes him or her feel uncomfortable, humiliated, or degraded. Mutual consent should be the password in the bedroom. What might this mean in terms of specifics? Almost anything as long as the decision is embraced by both spouses. You want whipped cream? Costumes? Toes? Enjoy—as long as both partners are in agreement.

Avoid Habits That Would Diminish Sexual Intimacy with Your Husband

Another guideline can be found in 1 Corinthians 7:2–5 where couples are instructed *not to deprive each other of sexual intimacy.* What might this mean specifically? Let me give you two examples of danger zones you may want to avoid.

One of the modes of sexual expression about which God is silent is the *M*-word: masturbation, or as it is sometimes called, self-pleasure. One of the dangers of masturbation is the temptation for it to become an easy replacement for the task of emotional and physical intimacy between a husband and wife. A habit of solo masturbation by either husband or wife can indeed deprive a spouse of sexual energy and attention that is rightfully his or hers.

I'd like to describe for you a second scenario that falls into this same category. I recently interviewed a woman who, several years ago, asked her husband to incorporate a vibrator into their lovemaking. What began as a harmless new experience led gradually into a dependence that has made lovemaking a less than intimate endeavor for this couple. This woman admitted that she no longer enjoys sex with her husband without the assistance of the vibrator, and that her husband is frustrated by the new direction their lovemaking has taken. For this couple, marital intimacy has been sacrificed to the god of physical sensations, and their marriage is suffering as a result.

Avoid Fantasizing about Individuals Other than Your Husband

Whether you are tempted to fantasize about a coworker or lose yourself in the pages of a lusty romance novel, your thought life impacts your relationships with your husband and with God as well. Matthew 5:28, in fact, makes it clear that mental infidelity is tantamount to actual adultery.

This is, in fact, a second danger linked with masturbation, since masturbation is often *linked with fantasies about individuals other than a spouse.* Yet as long as these two guidelines are not violated, I believe there are certain circumstances under which masturbation can have a place,

Pornography isn't confined to backstreet theaters and magazines in brown wrappers.

guiltlessly, in a Christian marriage. For example, engaging in self-stimulation with your partner, as a facet of foreplay, is one possibility. I also believe that, if couples are separated from each other by, say, a business trip or other travel, masturbation can provide an occasional and temporary outlet for pent-up sexual feelings if, of course, it is linked with thoughts of a spouse rather than fueled by thoughts or pictures of individuals outside your marriage.

Additionally, many experts prescribe masturbation for women who have a difficult time experiencing orgasm. *This is not done for the purpose of replacing sexual intimacy with a husband,* but as a way of helping a woman learn precisely what "works" for her, so that she can incorporate this valuable information into her marriage relationship. It makes sense to me! By exploring her own body, a woman can adjust her technique in response to subtle nuances of sensation. She can, in effect, learn what kind of touch she finds most stimulating and *then communicate this information to her husband.* By "practicing" alone for an initial and limited period of time, she can actually teach her body to become more responsive, which will in turn enrich the intimacy she experiences with her spouse.

Again, consider scriptural guidelines. Don't rely on masturbation in a way that deprives your husband of sexual attention, and don't fuel your libido with thoughts of other men or situations outside your marriage. Keeping these guidelines in mind, there is no scriptural prohibition regarding masturbation.

Don't Fill Your Mind with Myths and Lies about Sexuality

Yet another guideline for biblical sexuality might be found in 1 Corinthians 13:6 where we learn that "Love . . . does not rejoice in iniquity, but rejoices in the truth."

Unfortunately, the media rarely offers us the truth about healthy sexuality as it was intended by God. Instead, our society is obsessed with the propagation of myths and lies about sex. It is impossible to entirely avoid the world's view of sexuality. But we can be discriminating, and we can guard our minds and spirits from a constant barrage of half-truths and outright fiction. I know of some women who are virtually addicted to romance novels. There are other individuals or couples who make a steady diet out of sexually explicit movies, rated R or otherwise. Without condemning every romance novel or every R-rated movie, I must say that these modes of entertainment can encourage illicit fantasies and also fill our heads with twisted perceptions of sexuality as it was intended by God.

I believe daytime talk shows can also fit into this category. Occasionally they may provide a brief distraction from the stress of our day-to-day lives, but the danger lies in the fact that if we are not careful they can begin to negatively influence the way we think about life and relationships.

Avoid Addictions of the Flesh

Galatians 5:16 instructs you and me to walk in the Spirit so that we won't fulfill the lusts of the flesh. The following verses go on to describe how our flesh lusts for things that are in contrast to what the Spirit wants for us. If we satisfy these lusts, we will soon find ourselves in a tightly clinched trap, unable to do the things we know are right!

I believe this is one of the many verses in the Bible that can be used to address the dangers of pornography. Pornography is habit forming; it is an open doorway to an addiction that is potently difficult to break.

In addition, all of the other verses we've looked at in this chapter can be applied to pornography as well. First Corinthians 13:6, for example, tells us that "Love . . . does not rejoice in iniquity, but rejoices in the truth"—but pornography presents a grossly distorted image of sexuality in which little or no truth is represented. Matthew

An objective of sexuality is to deepen the magical bond between man and wife.

5:28 warns us against committing mental adultery, and yet pornography encourages fantasies of sex outside of marriage. First Corinthians 7:5 instructs husbands and wives not to deprive each other of sexual attention, and yet pornography diverts sexual attention and energy from our spouses.

You may be thinking that as long as you don't frequent sleazy adult theaters, these paragraphs can't possibly apply to you, but pornography is hardly confined to back-street theaters and magazines in brown wrappers! Today many R-rated movies contain material which a decade ago would have garnered an X-rating. Many romance novels can be pornographic as well. If you are in doubt about something you are about to read or watch, hold it up to the standard described in Philippians 4:8 where we are encouraged to fill our minds with things that are true, noble, right, pure, lovely, admirable, excellent, and praiseworthy.

Enjoy a Full Range of Sexual Expression with Your Husband

Yet another guideline for biblical sexuality can be derived from Hebrews 13:4, where we find the words, "Marriage is honorable among all, and the bed undefiled; but fornicators and adulterers God will judge."

What kind of sexual activity draws the judgment of God? Sex outside of marriage. On the other hand, marriage and the marriage bed are "honorable" and "undefiled." God is not standing as judge and jury over the sexuality you and I share with our husbands. What we choose to do—as long as it is not in conflict with other scriptural principles or edicts—is honorable. Undefiled. Experimenting with positions, technique, places, clothing, role-playing, sexual aids such as lotions or oils—these are honorable and undefiled. If it is something you and your husband agree, together, to incorporate into your lovemaking . . . well, more power to you.

Acknowledge and Protect the Mystery of Sexual Intimacy in Your Marriage

The last guideline is taken from several places in Scripture. It has to do with the mystery of the sexual and emotional union of a man and woman in marriage. Consider, for example, Ephesians 5:31, "For this reason a man shall leave his father and mother and be joined to his wife, and the two shall become one flesh."

How about Proverbs 30:18–19: "There are three things which are too wonderful for me, yes, four which I do not understand: The way of an eagle in the air, the way of a serpent on a rock, the way of a ship in the midst of the sea, and the way of a man with a virgin."

There is a mystery inherent in the intimate, vulnerable exchange that takes place in the most private moments of a marriage. This mystery is at the very heart of sexuality between husband and wife.

I think it is a wonderful thing for a husband and wife to explore many facets of sexual expression together. In the previous section I mentioned the freedom we have been given to experiment with positions, technique, clothing, and more! It's okay to cut loose, to have fun, to explore new frontiers, to relinquish some of the inhibitions that in reality have no basis in Scripture.

At the same time, let's not forget what is at the heart of lovemaking.

In the eighth chapter of 1 Corinthians, Paul talks about the fact that it is lawful for him to make certain choices, such as to eat meat that has been sacrificed to idols, and yet his freedom of choice is not as important as his relationship with others who might be offended by that choice. Relationships take precedence over liberties.

At the heart of lovemaking is the relationship we share with our husbands. Liberties are great—as long as they enhance that relationship. If and when they begin, in any way, to detract, we may need to make some adjustments.

The foundational purpose of lovemaking is not the pursuit of incredible sensations. Although incredible sensations are part of the package (and a pretty nice perk at that), an even greater objective of our sexuality is to deepen the magical, intimate bond between man and wife by sharing experiences, creating memories, exploring vulnerabilities, and probing the physical and emotional nooks and crannies that make us who we are.

If you feel uncomfortable about something, don't do it. If you and your husband want to try something new—and there is no scriptural cause for hesitation—then why not pray and seek God's blessing on your endeavor?

Thank him for the gift of your sexuality and the many facets of expression that are available to you. Ask him to steer you toward experiences that will enhance the pleasure and intimacy of marriage, and to guide you well clear of any experience that might diminish intimacy with your husband or entice either one of you into an area of sin.

Zealously Guard Your Marriage

There's something to be said for rules.

This is a difficult admission for me to make since I have always been partial to the adage that rules are made to be broken.

I am, in fact, a strict advocate of nonstructure. Especially in the kitchen. When I serve a meal, it is not unusual for my husband to tentatively raise the question, "Is there a recipe for this or did you make this up?" I say *tentatively* because he has learned the hard way that I am not fond of this question. I am not fond of this question because it implies that what I have just served him would never make it past Betty Crocker's product development department. I am not fond of this question because—if I were to ever answer truthfully (which, of course, will never actually happen)—I would have to admit that the meal I am serving could very well be the one exception to Solomon's "nothing new under the sun" philosophy.

Most of the meals I serve are, indeed, made up. Except my husband doesn't know this. Oh, he knows *instinctively,* but he has never wheedled an admission out of me. This is because whenever he asks me to fess up between "recipe" or "made up," I change the subject. To date, he has asked this question 157 times, and he has yet to receive a straight answer. He has learned, instead, a variety of useful tidbits regarding garbage disposal repair and spaying dogs and discreet hair removal techniques for women. I'm beginning to think he doesn't care if the meal is made up or not—I suspect he's pumping me for information for a book he's writing on the sly entitled *Revolting Dinner-Table Trivia.*

Just between you and me, yes, I wing it in the kitchen. And, I guess to some extent, in life. I get a certain thrill out of tweaking a guideline just a bit and watching to see what happens. Sometimes I am pleasantly surprised. Sometimes I am just . . . well, surprised.

As much as I like to bend the rules, in my lifetime I have made a profound discovery. I have stumbled across a number of guidelines that are not the enemies I once thought them to be. In fact, these rules don't complicate and restrict my life at all. On the contrary, they simplify and streamline my life. These guidelines are, in reality, my friends.

For example, I have discovered that there are helpful rules when it comes to finances. One of my financial rules for a simpler life is to use a check register. I know about this now because I used to use the long-term memory approach until I discovered that those bounced check charges can really take a bite out of your budget.

There are also rules for grocery shopping. For instance, I happen to know by trial and error that there are certain foods that run a high risk of not making it intact from the checkout stand to my front door. This is the reason I NEVER buy pecan praline ice cream or those frosted raisin cookies with the colored sprinkles—except, of course, at gunpoint, which has only happened once or twice and only in Los Angeles.

I even have rules for buying socks. No matter how good the sale, I never buy socks anywhere but Target. I never buy anything except one brand of sock, and I never buy any color but white or black. My order goes something like this: men's white athletic socks, men's black dress socks, girls' white athletic socks (for Kaitlyn). When I do laundry, it doesn't matter if a few socks are sacrificed to appease the hungry appliance gods (what else could it be when ten socks go in and only six come back out?). When the socks come out of the dryer I don't have to sort them by searchlight to distinguish the subtle nuances of color and pattern. I don't have to play matchmaker, either. No monogamous pairs allowed: Our socks go into drawers as a pile of swinging singles and come out with a different partner each time. Finally, I don't have to wonder if a sock belongs to Larry or to me; I wear the same ones he does (although not before washing).

If there are rules for something as trivial as buying socks, there must *certainly* be some guidelines for something as all-encompassing as our sexuality.

Protect the Institution That Protects Your Sexuality

Do you appreciate the gift of sexuality and enjoy expressing that gift? When it comes to the fullest possible sexual expression, the best guideline I can think of is to protect that sexuality by keeping it safely ensconced in a healthy, happy marriage.

Society today tells a different story. Society today says that when you try to confine sex to marriage alone, you're placing unnecessary boundaries on sexuality. Believe it or not, people today are dying of AIDS and getting abortions and raising kids scarred by the divorce of unfaithful parents . . . and still touting the message that subjecting sex to the confines of marriage is an archaic and dangerous restriction.

Which is exactly how I used to think of check registers. Now I know better.

Marriage is not the enemy. It is, in fact, the best friend your sexuality will ever have. Which leads me to the following questions: How can we protect our marriages? What guidelines can simplify, streamline, and even safeguard the institution that safeguards our sexuality?

Wedding Advice Best Served with a Pinch of Salt

At the dinner reception following our wedding, Larry and I made a request of our guests. We provided each guest with a three-by-five index card and asked for a "recipe" for a strong and happy marriage. Fortunately for you (or unfortunately, as the case may be), I still have all two hundred cards and would like to take this moment to share a few words of wisdom from the friends and family of the Scalfs and the Linamens.

One relative penned, with her tongue securely in her cheek (we hope): "I'd give you some good advice, but it's too late—you're already married." Another guest (probably her husband) wrote simply: "Duck and weave."

Other guests gave practical guidelines for spousal etiquette, such as "Keep your feet warm," and "Don't leave hair in the sink," and "Don't clear your throat or spit in front of your mate." Then there's my personal favorite: "Never eat breakfast in rollers—that goes for you, too, Karen!"

Finally, family friend Dale Collins shared this poignant advice: "Larry, give your wife all the credit—just make sure you keep the cash."

Okay, so maybe it's a good thing none of these people are marriage counselors. Nevertheless, I believe that there are plenty of solid guidelines that can help you protect and enhance your marriage. There are certainly more than the five I am going to outline in the following paragraphs, but these will serve as a nice representative sample. You'll notice that I organized these guidelines around the acronym GUARD because I believe that's what they can help you do. They can help guard your marriage against the barrage of divisions, distractions, and temptations that you and your husband face, no doubt, on a daily basis.

Guard Your Thoughts and Words

Our thoughts determine our attitudes and our actions. At the risk of oversimplifying the matter, the battle to protect your marriage from disillusionment, bitterness, and even affairs may well be waged and won, first and foremost, in your mind.

And when it comes to the fruit of our lips . . . well, contrary to that old sticks and stones philosophy, words *do* hurt. Make a conscious effort to wield your words and thoughts as tools to protect and fortify your marriage and your husband, rather than to destroy and tear down.

Undergird Your Marriage with Prayer

There may be some truth to the saying that couples that pray together, stay together. Coming together in prayer before a holy God isn't easy. Prayer requires a level of vulnerability and transparency that can be intimidating for many couples. Yet the rewards are great. In their book *If Two Shall Agree* (Revell, 1992) Carey Moore and Pam Rosewell Moore talk about the adventure they embarked on when they began, during courtship and on into marriage, to pray together every day. One of the benefits they reaped was a new focus on consideration toward each other and for people outside their marriage as well. As Carey writes, "I cannot be careless or insensitive in what I say to Pam and then pray with her. Nor can either of us treat anyone else rudely or engage in gossip and criticism, or allow conceit and pride to rule our relations with others, and expect God to hear our prayers at the end of the day."

Pray with your spouse. Pray for your spouse. Pray for a strong and godly marriage. I promise you that your prayers will be heard. How can I say that? Simple. According to 1 John 5:14–15: "This is the assurance we

Our marriages don't have to be average.

have in approaching God: that if we ask anything according to his will, he hears us. And if we know that he hears us—whatever we ask—we know that we have what we asked of him" (NIV). Is it God's will for your marriage to be vibrant and healthy, a shining example of all that God intended the institution of marriage to be? Of course. Then as you pray according to his will, know that your prayers have been heard, and that he is working on your behalf.

Assess Your Marriage Frequently

There are few guarantees in life, but one of them is that from time to time you and your husband are going to drift apart on the sea of love. How can you tell when this happens? Well, you know you might be drifting when you plan a dinner party for your closest friends and discover you've forgotten to invite your spouse. Or when you turn on the radio, hear the first few bars of "You've Lost That Loving Feeling," and catch yourself saying, "Hey, honey! They're playing our song!" Or when your anniversary rolls around and *both* of you forget.

There is no way to avoid those times when stress, children, work, illness, familiarity, boredom—basically, life in general!—conjoin to weaken the bond between husband and wife. The key is in knowing what to do when it happens.

Make a list of the warning signs. What symptoms clue you in to the fact that your relationship is not the priority that it should be? These might be emotions, such as feeling lonely, isolated, stressed-out, or distracted. They might also be behaviors, such as maintaining separate bedtimes or developing friends in different circles.

In addition to watching for warning signals, you might want to establish specific times for you and your husband to get together and assess your relationship. It might be a "date night" once a week or even once a month, or perhaps you'll agree to attend a marriage seminar once each year. You might even look for informal moments, such as a walk in the park or along a beach, to look each other in the eyes and say, "How are we doing?"

Now, create a game plan detailing strategies to help you get back on track. Have in hand, ahead of time, a few ideas that can "prime the pump" the next time you and your husband are in need of some marriage maintenance. What helps bring you back in sync with each other? It might be as simple as a night of attentive lovemaking. Or perhaps, over the course of a week or two, meeting several times for lunch away from the phone and the bills and the kids. A marriage retreat weekend might even be in order, or perhaps even a few sessions with a marriage counselor.

The key is to keep a finger on the pulse of your marriage, and to take quick action if you have any questions about the health of your relationship.

Relinquish Small Hurts

Misunderstandings, hurt feelings, insensitive remarks or actions . . . well, they're pretty inevitable in any relationship as day-to-day and intimate as the one shared by husband and wife. Occasionally, of course, some really big conflict will thunder like a rolling boulder between you and your husband. But most of the time, it is the long-term accumulation of a mother lode of small stuff—the pebbles, rocks, and irritating grains of marital discord—that can eventually create a treacherous mountain between even the most tender lovers.

So how can we avoid amassing a major mountain out of small hurts and wounds? I asked a number of married couples how they do it. Here's a sampling of their suggestions.

> "Learn how to see the humor in life—especially when you're mad at your husband. You can find some hu-

morous element in almost any fight, and after a good laugh, it's harder to stay mad."

"I saw a TV show once where a fictional married couple made a pact that whenever they had a serious argument they had to strip and argue in the nude. The thought was, of course, that they would end up making love instead of war. I don't know how it would work in real life, but I'd certainly be willing to give it a try."

"If I'm feeling peeved or hurt over some small thing, I tell myself to forget it and go on. If I can't let go of it quite yet, I give myself a small window of time in the future in which to feel sorry for myself. For instance, I might earmark next Tuesday morning between 10:00 and 11:00 as my hour in which to have myself a pity party. Knowing that I have a 'date' in which to exercise my feelings of anger or hurt sometimes allows me to set those feelings aside until then. Usually by the time my 'window' rolls around, I'm ready to forgive and forget."

"Every now and then I approach my husband and ask him if there's anything I've done, knowingly or unknowingly, to offend him or leave him feeling angry, hurt, or diminished in some way. If he's been bothered by some incident or comment, he tells me, and I ask him to forgive me. Prompted by my example, he'll usually follow up by asking me if there's anything he's done to hurt me. The key is not to try to defend yourself when it's your spouse's turn to talk. Don't justify. It doesn't matter if, on the day you snapped at your husband in front of his friends, you were freaking out because you'd just discovered your son got his tongue pierced. Regardless of your motivations, your husband was embarrassed, and an apology will go a long way to salve frayed emotions."

"Sometimes I ask myself if I'm expecting Jeff to be too perfect. When I get mad at some small thing, I wonder how I would feel if I had to be as perfect as I expect him to be."

"I used to let resentment build in my silence. Now I say to my husband, with an attitude of vulnerability rather than accusation, *I felt bad when you said or did* . . . And a lot of times he's surprised because he had no idea his words or actions had the impact that they did."

Defy the Odds

One book that I read estimated that out of any dozen married couples, four end up in front of a divorce lawyer, six stay together without love or joy for the sake of their children, careers, or religious beliefs, and only two couples enjoy an intimate and happy marriage.

Not a pretty picture, I'll admit. But luckily for you and me, the destiny of our marriages rests not with statistic-mongers, but in our own hands. Our choices, priorities, and commitments are even now determining the quality of our marriages today and on into the future.

What a privilege and responsibility!

Our marriages don't have to die a statistical death. They don't have to be average. They don't have to become utilitarian institutions in which the words "You're hogging the blanket" pass for intimate pillow talk. We can be in that 2 percent. We can experience intimate marriages. We can defy the odds.

But here's the rub. All the things we're looking for in our marriages—emotional intimacy, soul-to-soul bonding, companionship, romance, and . . . come on, admit it

. . . great sex—take a little planning. None of it happens by accident. An emotionally and sexually intimate union requires a conscious effort (and I do hope you understand I'm not referring merely to staying awake during sex).

Think of it sort of like . . . well, like a diet pill. A couple years ago I saw a TV ad for some new miracle diet pill. The testimonials were glowing. The models were gorgeous. The claims were attention-grabbers. Even the price was reasonable. In fact, for less than thirty bucks I was promised the easiest, fastest weight loss in the history of cellulite. And everything was guaranteed. If I didn't reach my desired weight virtually faster than I could say "Jack Sprat," I'd get my money back and I would even get to keep the handy seven-day plastic pill dispenser. (The dispenser was plastic, not the pills.)

Nothing could be easier. In fact, I think the product was even named E-Z something-or-other. Naturally, this should have been my first clue: Never trust a company that cannot correctly spell out the name of its product. Of course, it could have been worse: The E-Z Diet Pill could have been named by someone even less literate and called something like W8 B-Gone.

My point is that I actually had a momentary brain-glitch and considered dialing the 800-number on the screen—but then something caught my attention in the lower left corner of my TV screen. It was more than a fingerprint, bigger than a smudge, but not by much. Probably some remnant of the seamier side of family life—you know, like a swirl of dog saliva or a strand of bubblegum. That's when I leaned in for a closer look and discovered . . . small print.

Or should I say small print?

That's right. In four-point type, the manufacturers of the E-Z W8 B-Gone 1-der drug were telling me something important I needed to know about their product.

The small print said, "Guaranteed results are contingent on pills being used in conjunction with diet plan and exercise program."

What?

Where's the remote control? Better yet, get me a sledgehammer.

Diet and *exercise program?*

ALMOST ANYTHING WILL WORK WITH A DIET AND EXERCISE PROGRAM. Sugar pills will work with a diet and exercise program. Advil will make you lose weight with a diet and exercise program. M&Ms. Small buttons. Even plastic pills will work wonders—when teamed with a diet and exercise program!

I guess another dream bites the dust: There are no miracle pills. No weight-loss wonder drugs. No magic wands. No fairy dust. The small print said it all: _______ (fill in the blank with any nontoxic substance known to man) plus diet and exercise will reap rewards.

And all of this, of course, leads me back to marriage.

When I was single I used to think that all I needed to do to have a great marriage was find Mr. Right. My Miracle Man. E-Z Spouse. Wonder Husband. If I could just get my hands on the right hunk-o-man, intimacy would be effortless.

Now, of course, I know better.

Now I know that there are no magic marriages. No perfect-ten relationships. Now I understand that any marriage—in order to achieve its potential and become the celebration of intimacy that is God's gift to husbands and wives—must be teamed with some sacrifice and sweat.

Do you want to defy the odds? Do you want your marriage to be the best it can be? Do you want to experience lifelong emotional and physical intimacy with the man in your life? Then remember the small print. Quick fixes rarely last; instead, make an effort to learn the disciplines and principles that, practiced daily, will help shape your marriage into all that you want it to be and more.

Now You Know Your ABCs . . .

We've come a long way, you and I. From **A**sking and **B**eating and **C**elebrating to e**X**alting and saying **Y**es and guarding with **Z**eal, we have certainly become well-versed in matters of marital intimacy. Now comes the fun part as we strive to put these principles into daily practice in our relationships with our husbands.

Indeed, now that we know our ABCs, the opportunities are endless. Marriage is, after all, not unlike a library; tales of adventure and intrigue, comedy, tragedy, mystery, and romance are written daily in the pages of our lives as married women. Taking the time, as we have done, to become literate in the principles of intimacy is one of the best ways I know to ensure that plenty of poetry is included as well!

In closing, I'll be praying for you and your marriage, and if you think about it, say a quick prayer for me and mine. What a profound privilege and awesome adventure awaits us as we begin today to follow the ABCs to greater intimacy in our marriages.

You've been so patient and have listened to me for more than two hundred pages. Now, it's your turn! I'd love to hear from you. Drop me a line at:

Karen Linamen
P.O. Box 2673
Duncanville, TX 75138